Dear Dr Mrs Dupe Ayinisode,
I Pray that God gives
you Speed and grace by
this Book.
Every Blessings.

Chinkie Morsi
08.05.2016

D1743806

IF I WERE A
Mother

Chukie Morsi

authorHOUSE®

AuthorHouse™ UK
1663 Liberty Drive
Bloomington, IN 47403 USA
www.authorhouse.co.uk
Phone: 0800.197.4150

Scripture quotations marked KJV are from the Holy Bible, King James Version (Authorized Version). First published in 1611. Quoted from the KJV Classic Reference Bible, Copyright © 1983 by The Zondervan Corporation.

Scripture quotations marked AMP are from The Amplified Bible, Old Testament copyright © 1965, 1987 by the Zondervan Corporation. The Amplified Bible, New Testament copyright © 1954, 1958, 1987 by The Lockman Foundation. Used by permission. All rights reserved.

Scripture quotations marked GNT are taken from the Good News Translation — Second Edition. Copyright © 1992 by American Bible Society. Used by permission. All rights reserved.

Published by AuthorHouse 12/02/2015

ISBN: 978-1-5049-9556-6 (sc)
ISBN: 978-1-5049-9557-3 (hc)
ISBN: 978-1-5049-9558-0 (e)

Library of Congress Control Number: 2015919646

Print information available on the last page.

Any people depicted in stock imagery provided by Thinkstock are models, and such images are being used for illustrative purposes only. Certain stock imagery © Thinkstock.

This book is printed on acid-free paper.

Cover Design: Faith Morsi
    FAITHGRAPHICS

Photograph: Emmanuella Morsi
    NOCTURNAL

The LOGO

The logo is a trademark of **CEFMORSI MINISTRIES INTERNATIONAL** in the United Kingdom and in countries where the Global Outreach Mission of **CEFMORSI MINISTRIES INTERNATIONAL** is welcome. All rights reserved and therefore must not be duplicated.

DEDICATION

I dedicate this book to my Mother - **Deaconess Victoria MORSI (nee Okoh),** my Wife - **Faith,** my Daughter - **Emmanuella** and to **All Mothers and Believers of All-Faith in Christ Jesus,** who quest, pant and long after more of God.

APPRECIATION

I sincerely appreciate my son Joshua who assisted in the typing of the transcript. I also appreciate my lovely wife Faith, for the editorial proof-reading and book cover design. And to the best of all, the four gracious boys in my life: Daniel, Joshua, Joel (Ozzie) and Zachary, for all their help at various times especially my sweet daughter Emmanuella. I am absolutely grateful.

ACKNOWLEDGEMENT

I'm highly indebted to several people I've had personal encounters and fellowship with at various times and in various ways, whose lives at various stages in those encounters, contributed towards the making and publishing of this book: **Firstly,** my mother in-law Mrs Seddy Nyathi and Sisters-in-law, Mrs Helen Morsi, Mrs Gladys Morsi, Mrs Bridget O. Morsi, Miss Nompu Nyathi; Mrs Patricia Ncube and Mrs Felicia Mormah. **Secondly,** my Siblings: Eunice Olokor (Mrs), Vera Aghedo (Mrs), Beatrice Igwe (Mrs), Katherine Obuh (Mrs) and Benedicta Obanor (Mrs). **Thirdly, my Ministerial friends:** Pastor (Dr) Christian Kumbi, Pastor (Mrs) Mary Okpewho-Udume, Minister (Mrs) Eunice Ezewu, Evangelist Mrs Sarah Ighalo, Revd Debbie T. Adedeji, Pastor Mrs Debbie Adeshina, Chyto Ike-Egbuonu (Mrs) and Minister (Mrs) Eunice Nwaki; **My Lovely Aunties and Mothers** - Mama Preye Koroye, Mama Regina Odeh, Mrs Clara Biu, Barrister Tayo Aina (Mrs), Chief Mrs Beatrice Ewah, Mama Vashti Lewis, Mama Modupe Ariyibi and Ms Norma Mkandia; **My Beloved Friends in Christ** – Mrs Margaret Evarie, Deaconess Mrs Sarah Okpewho, Mrs Patience Esim, Mrs Oluranti Ojo, Deaconess Mrs Mabel Komoni, Stella Egwuonwu (Mrs), Peace Igodifo (Mrs), Grace Odumuzor (Mrs), Ms Betty Singa-Fanu, Boma E. Nemi (Mrs), Furo Sofia (Ms), Fatola Alice (Mrs), Ufuoma Igho Okpubuluku-Ogefere, Jenny N. Ogidi (Mrs), Kemi Obakin (Mrs), Faustina Hammond (Mrs), Lisa Van Derberg (Mrs), Trish Jones (Mrs), Kemi Oladapo (Mrs) and Rosa Ileyesa-Munanga (Mrs), Dr Mrs Dupe Ayorinde,

Tilly Gbolahun-Majek (Mrs), Mrs Nse Udoh, Ms Comfort Auta, Mrs Sayo Kudehinbu and many more, filled-up in my hearts, too numerous for which I am grateful to God on my personal encounter with them.

COMMENDATION
Acts 20:32

*"So now, brethren, **I commend you** to God and to the word of His grace, which is able to build you up and give you an inheritance among all those who are sanctified"*

CONSCIENCE
Acts 24:16

*"This being so, I myself always strive to have a **conscience** without offense toward God and men."*

THE KNOWING OF CHRIST
Philippians 3:9-14

"And be found in Him, not having my own righteousness, which is from the law, but that which is through faith in Christ, the righteousness which is from God by faith; [10] ***that I may know Him and the power of His resurrection, and the fellowship of His sufferings, being conformed to His death,*** [11] *if, by any means, I may attain to the resurrection from the dead.* [12] *Not that I have already attained, or am already perfected; but I press on, that I may lay hold of that for which Christ Jesus has also laid hold of me.* [13] *Brethren, I do not count myself to have apprehended; but one thing I do, forgetting those things which are behind and reaching forward to those things which are ahead,* [14] *I press toward the goal for the prize of the upward call of God in Christ Jesus."*

Oh Lord!

In your name, may the longings and spirit yearnings of my heart, go with this book to awaken the individual in faith and spirit, and to strengthen your Church with inspiration, revelation and empowerment. And by the effectual working of the Holy Spirit in the living Word of God, that through this book they may know you as the only true God and Jesus Christ whom you have sent, for this is life eternal, as in the scripture of John 17:3. Thank you Lord, Amen.

I DO PRAY THAT YOU MAY ALWAYS REMEMBER:
THAT BEING A MOTHER IS NOT NECESSARILY ABOUT
WHAT YOU GAVE UP TO HAVE A CHILD, BUT WHAT
YOU'VE GAINED IN AND FROM HAVING ONE

CONTENTS

FIRST WORDS

Being Founded In Faith!

Being Founded In FAITH:

May I begin by attributing my thanks to God for what the Holy Spirit has done and is doing in my generation in the lives of many women, especially mothers, in stepping up in grace to the challenges of this generation. The book 'If I Were A mother' is relevant or will be relevant only to those who are founded or desire to be founded in the faith of the creator of the person called a mother or of motherhood, even our Lord God through Jesus Christ our Lord.

In the course of these acts of the Holy Spirit, I have found that by the privilege of being God's servant and minister of the gospel of the timeless book of life, some mothers are not fully rooted, founded and established in their faith in our Lord Jesus Christ; This realisation compelled me to write this book in line with **Colossians 2:7** which speaks of the need to be rooted and to grow in Christ and to have our lives built on him. This way, because of the truth that has been taught - our faith will grow strong. As a result of this deficiency of the knowing and understanding in relating to godly motherhood in child bearing and raising them accordingly, many have struggled and are still struggling today to incorporate motherhood and godly living, especially with the challenges of absent fathers, godly father's in some cases.

Psalms 11:3 says that, *"If the foundations be destroyed, what can the righteous do?"* This means that if the foundation of our faith is being destroyed, what else can the godly do; and I would argue that the righteous have to go back to the original manuscripts and the creator of that manuscript if restoration is to be witnessed again. I believe that this is possible with God. A mother's foundation of faith needs to be solid in order for her to be able to pass it on to her children. Jesus in the gospel of **Luke 6:46-49** and **Matthew 7:21-27** enjoins the Christian Faith believer who wants to succeed and triumph in dominion and have their building, *suffice to mean their faith*, not founded on the solid rock, will soon find out that their building will be swept away by the wind and storms of life. Many have being swept away. What an irony. This is why we see many Christian mothers and women, struggle in their faith most times, in the course of their trying to balance up their godly life and motherhood.

I know and understand the vitality of this act of being founded by faith to enhance ones goal; it's because of the changes and transformation that took place in my family when my mother gave her life and her all to Christ. She began to feed her spirit-being with the solid word of God and attend fellowship and Bible Study with a genuine Word-Based teaching Church where she built her faith in Christ and to living godly. As a result of this, my siblings and I were challenged to seek after God even more.

My mother's faith being founded on the truth, which is the word of God, changed her person and personality in the way she did things, in the way she spoke to and with us and in making life decisions. When her life began to relate to her beliefs, her ways of doing life with the family changed profoundly. We could literally see **Philippians 3:9, Jude 1:3** and **1 Peter 1:7** in her life and the acts of doing life and stuff. That fascinated me the more.

I pray that God would cause every mother or woman reading this book to be founded in their faith by knowledge and understanding to help change and transform lives. Blessed Reading,

Chukie MORSI Snr.

PREFACE

Introduction

This book 'If I Were A Mother' is a book of inspiration, revelation and empowerment. Its key objective is to ignite godly women to become achievers and to live triumphantly as Christian Mothers in Christ Jesus.

The inspiration to write this book came from my personal encounters in living with my Mother and from the many Mothers that I have been privileged to meet over time.

What I learnt from my Mother and these gracious mothers in the course of my growth in various stages in life has made me be what I am. The motherly experiences that have sharpened my life as a man by my godly, industrious, resourceful, diligent, virtuous, prudent, faithful, charming and understanding Mother could be summed up in this book. It's my privilege and intention to inspire, reveal and empower every mother to become what they want to be in their fulfilling of God's plans, purposes and pursuits. This counts for those that have adopted or are guardian to children. The result of this good intention is to make the good happen and to avert events of life that some have lived to regret as we see in the following scriptural truth.

Some examples, can be found in the following scriptural illustrations; **Proverbs 15:20** enables us to know that a wise son will make his father glad while a foolish one will despise his dear mother. He would undermine her and take her for granted; In **Proverbs 29:15** the scripture enjoins that by the rod and reproof which is instruction, wisdom is given to a child whereas a child left to himself will bring his mother to shame, embarrassment and reproach. Hence **Proverbs**

22:6 gives us responsibilities as parents, considering the context to train up our child in the way they should go. The idea is that the training of the child would guide them to maturity and they would then follow godly living through adulthood. Such was the exemplary responsibility imparted by Lois and Eunice, grandma and mother to Timothy in **2 Timothy 3:15.** Apostle Paul was reminding him that it was from early childhood that he had learnt the scriptures which then gave him the wisdom to receive the salvation that came because he trusted in Christ.

My dear blessed **Mother!** I present to you this special book in the precious name of our saviour and Lord Jesus Christ in whom we live, we move and we have our being - Amen! It beholds God in His grace to call you His people. *It's my prayer that by this book you might be inspired to aspire and not expire; that you might be illuminated and enlightened, receive revelation and graceful empowerment by the spirit of God — to the end you might excel, your dreams and aspirations in life might be fruitful and you can be a blessing to yourself, family, humanity and posterity without hindrance.* I also pray that you will find the goodwill of God to celebrate the love that MOTHERHOOD brings to family, society and our world, Amen!

I am specially constrained by the inspiration of the Holy Spirit to remind you that as a mother you are - **SPECIAL. All mothers are special irrespective of race, class and place.** My listening to the sayings of the Holy Spirit as in **Luke 1:45** below accorded and authenticated it the more in my passionate desire to write this book.

> *"Blessed is she who believed, for there will be a fulfillment of those things which were told her from the Lord."*

I want to let you know again and again in the context of **Luke 1:45,** that God is determined to bring your yearning desires to pass and to see fruitfulness, flourishing and fulfilment in all things He has spoken to you being a mother; and what He is speaking or will yet speak to you about, as you believe and act in His words accordingly.

Proverb 29:15 *"The rod and reproof give wisdom: but a child left to himself bringet his mother to shame (disgrace)."* *(Emphasis mine)*

To be a mother is an act of grace considering the scripture of **Proverbs 29:15** above. In that any woman can be a biological mother, but only a special heartfelt woman lives beyond being a child bearer but – **a Mother!** Motherhood is special and much more vital when you are a godly woman whose earnest desire is to please God by seeing God's purposes come to pass in your life, family and humanity. That is when your whole life totally depends on God's guidance, not mere wishful thoughts and concepts of human ideology. This is when God should not be considered as a last resort but the first port of call. God wants to bring about a glorious today and better tomorrow to our generation and posterity. Motherhood has a major part to play in bringing it to fruitfulness. **Will you Let God?**

IF I WERE A MOTHER!

Igniting The Godly Woman
To Become An Achiever & To Live Triumphantly

IF I WERE A MOTHER: *I Would Live A Godly & Blessed Life!*

There are blessings in living a godly life and it should be the greatest desire of any child and believer in Christ Jesus.

From reading **Luke 1:45,** one primary thing is evident – **Being Blessed.** Just as it written *"And blessed is she that believed for there shall be a performance of those things which were told her from the Lord.".* In the same grace, **1 Peter 3:5-9** indicates that we are called to inherit a blessing in the kingdom, every one of God's children even as it is also written: *"For after this manner in the old time the **holy (godly) women** also, who trusted in God, adorned themselves . . . and as being heirs together of the grace of life . . . Not rendering evil for evil, or railing for railing: **but contrariwise blessing; knowing that ye are thereunto called, that ye should inherit a blessing."***

The blessed mother is the woman who has entered a covenant of grace made available by our Lord Jesus Christ for all who will believe in Him. To be **blessed** means to be empowered to *succeed, achieve, become, bring forth or bring about positive results in one's life.* When someone says to you - *be blessed or God bless you or God's blessings –* they are invariably declaring you to be empowered to succeed, achieve, to make the impossible possible and to become the success that God has intended one to be. The blessing of God enriches and dispels sorrow. That's the amazing and awesomeness of God in all He does with us

His children. That's the truth, and in my simple paraphrased analogy of **Proverbs 10:2**, I convey it this way - **The *blessing of the Lord*,** it makes one rich, and God does not add any form of sorry with it at all. The blessing of the LORD is more than silver and gold, wealth and riches but it creates them into our lives when we live a godly life of God in us.

We must come to know that the achieving godly mother is empowered by God to succeed and triumph in life's endeavours as a - **woman, wife and mother**. It's a fact in society that not all mothers are wives but one thing is certain they are all called woman. She is a mother to a child or children born, fostered or adopted. A godly Christian mother is blessed to achieve greatness in life and have good success. **Joshua 1:8** and **Psalm 1:1-3** and **3 John 2** enjoin us to know that God's intent is to see us succeed, prosper and to achieve our aspirations in life and gracious desires and goals.

We see in **1 Peter 3:9** that the godly Christian woman – *Mother*- is called to inherit a blessing, and you are that woman. Just envision it, believe it and see yourself become the called one to inherit a blessing as it's written in the holy writ. When you can envision it, there's no limit or height that you can't attain with God. In **Galatians 3:13-14** the godly Christian woman **– mother –** is redeemed from curses to a blessed life. Do you think you are cursed or under a curse causing a stalemate in your life or engrossed with the circumstantial limitations you may be considering now? Start thinking different and accepting the new you in Christ Jesus, qualified and justified to access God's blessings because of what Christ Jesus has done, that is, He has redeemed you from curse to blessing. You are a blessed child of God.

The godly Christian mother is blessed simply because she is a believer in the entirety of God's word concerning her. We see this in **Luke 1:45**. If I were a mother – *godly woman* - I would live in the grace of God and in the consciousness that I am **redeemed and blessed**. This act of consciousness in one's daily life will liberate, give freedom and life worth to self, family, church, society, all and sundry. I hope you give in to what God's WORD says you are in Christ – a Godly woman, qualified and justified with blessings.

IF I WERE A MOTHER: *I Would Radiate Excellence In Virtue!*

I have come to understand through grace and experience to know that people of excellence and virtue attract others effortlessly. People love them and want to be around them, because excellence and virtue attract.

To **excel** means - to do well, to achieve, to be exceptional, to surpass, to be above limit, to stand out or be outstanding and superior and making a difference; while **virtue** has to do with goodness, that is, good behaviour, noble character, moral goodness, integrity and such likes good qualities in and of life.

These characteristics of virtues are what **Proverbs 31:10** endeavours to convey of the beautiful woman which you are. She is hard to find because she is priceless, she is above the most precious stones of all sorts – rubies as the stated: *"Who can find a virtuous woman? For her price is far above rubies".* More so, **Proverbs 31:29** indicates that many daughters of God have done excellently and virtuously; meaning it's all possible and not an extra task that you cannot attain or be as it's written: *"Many daughters have done virtuously, but thou excellest them all".* Further Scriptures in this light can be found of a wise woman like you in *Proverb 14:1 and Proverb 24:3-4* respectively, conveying to every woman and more to the godly Mother that they can excel with goodness in any endeavour they set their heart to accomplish.

If I were a woman, my priority would be to use my God given blessedness to radiate excellence in virtue. The proverbs thirty one woman happens to be a mother with outstanding virtue. She is worth knowing and emulating if we must bring about the desired change in our life, family and society at large. One key issue about this woman is that she is not just any kind of woman but an excellent woman in virtue – **Goodness**. She is blessed – *empowered to succeed* – and she lives this out. I believe that if I were a mother, I would be the new creation woman for the new creation Church.

There is a heart cry today in families, the church and society at large for true motherhood. Betrayers are found in homes, the church and society today where children have been abandoned and some lack proper parental care; hence they live with broken spirits and emotional heartbreak. It's a damaging issue of many lives today, considering the rate of divorce among Christians. What is heart-breaking is that the children become the proverbial ground under which these two parental elephants are fighting. There are the victims. Parental instability may damage the child's ability to trust in God fully in spite of the respective individual explanations which they find difficult to comprehend. This individualistic selfishness for whatever reasons only ends up crushing the child's faith in God.

The proverbial mother's daily effort is to excel in virtue – *goodness* – by the blessedness – *empowerment* – she has received to succeed. She chooses to be the wise woman and mother of *Proverb 14:1 and Proverb 24:3-4*, who through knowledge and understanding will wisely bring up her child/children graciously well; such that it will give worth to their lives, the society and of course the churches of God on earth.

IF I WERE A MOTHER: *I Would Pursue God in His Abounding Grace To Excel!*

Excelling in virtue is an act of the grace of God made available to us by our Lord Jesus Christ. **What then is grace or rather abounding grace?** Without being theological, let me give us what I do know and understood grace or abounding grace to be:

- Grace is the free gift of God.
- Grace is God beaming His loving-kindness upon you in the midst of absolute sins and rejection by all.
- Grace is God showing you mercy, peace and favour when you should have being condemned.
- Grace is God's riches at Christ's expense.
- Grace is the capacity to forgive oneself, forgive others while accepting God's forgiveness.
- Grace is the capacity and enabling presence of God to do the seemingly possible and impossible to any mankind.
- Grace is the capacity to live in the freedom which God has afforded you in Christ, that is, wherein Christ has set you free and not engaging in other practices that lead to bondage.
- Grace is the divine endowment and enthronement that enable you to live triumphantly and victoriously in the midst of calculated opposition and more.
- Grace is God's unmerited favour over your life that can't be bought by any earthly or demonic medium of exchange except by the simple faith in God through Christ Jesus.
- Grace is the capacity and enabling help of God to love the lovable and unlovable without prejudice.
- Grace is God reaching out to man for the good of man.
- Grace is God's capacity to make man rule and reign in dominion over the elements of sin and its effect in the world.
- Grace is God, working out the human daily redemption in Christ Jesus from the forces of wickedness.
- Grace is you enjoying God and His providence effortless and stress free.
- Grace is Christ Jesus in you, the hope of glory.
- Grace is of the acts and processes in the redemption of mankind.

We know and understand that grace is God's kindness shown towards people because He loves them; and grace is the enabling from on high which is beyond human ability and capacity. God's free gift given to us without our involvement; I say that the acronym of **GRACE** is *God's Riches At Christ's Expense*. Grace is the God's power, anointing, favour and endowment at work in our life to do life and excel exceedingly beyond us in every capacity.

You can only picture what God's grace is all about when you consider the Scriptures say in **John 15:5.** *"I am the vine, ye are the branches: He that abideth in me, and I in him, the same bringeth forth much fruit: for without me ye can do nothing"*. This timeless scriptural truth indicates how much we can do with God in Christ Jesus and how we cannot become what we intend to be without Him, His eternal plans, purposes and pursuits. (Further reading can be found in **2 Timothy 1:9**).

The enrichment of how important we dearly desire and would have to live by grace in God is indicated in **Ephesians 2:8-10,** which speaks of the grace of God being a gift from God. That it was God's intended purpose for you to live godly in Christ through this grace that one does not need to work for whatsoever. It is available to the child of God. This scripture in Ephesians accords us on the gracious opportunity to succeed and do well and whole as God's workmanship. Success, fulfillment and excellence is in the grace of God accomplished in Christ Jesus. To succeed is to be empowered by the grace of God. This means that for a virtuous mother to achieve, succeed and be fulfilled, she needs the grace available from the Godhead as the scripture of **2 Corinthians 13:14** sums it up. *"The grace of the Lord Jesus Christ, and the love of God, and the communion of the Holy Ghost, be with you all. Amen"*. This scripture in second Corinthians indicates that excelling in virtue as a godly mother, one needs to make Jesus Christ the Lord of their life; the Holy Spirit has to be your general overseer, and the Father God has to be positioned as Father indeed in all life decisions in order for there to be any accomplishment. He will only commend what He commands and approves. Excelling in virtue is about doing life for the good of our well-being, family, church and society at large.

IF I WERE A MOTHER: *I Would Be Planted In God & In His House!*

To be planted in anything worth living or dying for means to be deeply rooted; firmly fixed or held in place. It is refreshing and gracious to know God in Christ Jesus early in one's life. One great priesthood prayer of Jesus for His disciples firstly and all is of **John 17:3** which says *"And this is life eternal, that they might know thee the only true God, and Jesus Christ, whom thou hast sent"*. This shows how much Christ Jesus wants all to be planted in God and also in His house.

I can recall that privileged opportunity that God gave to me which I strongly desire for any child because the character formation and the person it made me become to offer to my children and those around me; Today I can look back to it and say thank you Lord.

This is the experience of Timothy from his mother Eunice and Grandmother Lois according to **2 Timothy 1: 3-7** which Apostle Paul recalled to Timothy of his excellent spirit and unfeigned faith: *"I thank God, whom I serve from my forefathers with pure conscience, that without ceasing I have remembrance of thee in my prayers night and day; 4 greatly desiring to see thee, being mindful of thy tears, that I may be filled with joy; 5 when I call to remembrance the unfeigned faith that is in thee, which dwelt first in thy grandmother Lois, and thy mother Eunice; and I am persuaded that in thee also. 6 Wherefore I put thee in remembrance that thou stir up the gift of God, which is in thee by the putting on of my hands. 7 For God hath not given us the spirit of fear; but of power, and of love, and of a sound mind".*

For a child whose mother is planted in the house of God, there is a sense of security amidst the turmoil that the world sees today. My mother is such a woman and I am grateful to God for that. In such an environment I was able to see God and experience Him as **Isaiah 61:1-3** would counsel and enjoin one of having the Holy Spirit resting upon them. *"The Spirit of the Lord God is upon me; because the Lord hath anointed me to preach good tidings unto the meek; he hath sent me to bind up the brokenhearted, to proclaim liberty to the captives, and the opening of the prison to them that are bound; 2 to proclaim the acceptable year of the Lord, and the day of vengeance of our God; to comfort all that mourn; 3 to appoint unto them that mourn in Zion, to give unto them beauty for ashes, the oil of joy for mourning, the garment of praise for the spirit of heaviness; that they might be called trees of righteousness, the planting of the Lord, that he might be glorified."*

My mother was my backbone of hope and strength to serve God in Christ Jesus by the Holy Spirit. In her I saw the need to be planted in order to flourish in God rather than being a potted plant that is never steady. In **Psalms 1:1-3** it states *"Blessed is the man that walketh not in the counsel of the ungodly, nor standeth in the way of sinners, nor sitteth in the seat of the scornful. 2But his delight is in the law of the LORD; and in his law doth he meditate day and night. 3And he shall be like a tree planted by the rivers of water, that bringeth forth his fruit in his season; his leaf also shall not wither; and whatsoever he doeth shall prosper"*. **Psalms 92:12-15** in affirmation with Psalms one, ensures that only the planted and not the potted can flourish in God. Meaning there's no place in God for rolling stones. We need to be stable in God's grace and presence so that by being planted in His grace presence and house of worship, He can show us the path of life in order to enjoy His pleasures effortlessly as He indeed indicates to accomplish for His people in **Psalms 16:11** and **Psalms 35:27.**

When mothers are planted in God's house and in His Word by the Holy Spirit, there is no force that can stop them from prospering, flourishing and blossoming in God's love. They would achieve their desired goals with pleasure, they will be fruitful and flourish as the previous scriptures have stated and in **John 15:1-8, 16.** This act of fruitfulness and flourishing I have seen and witness in many mothers that I have had the privilege to be close to.

John 15:1-8 & 16 indicates the various progressive stages of fruitfulness as a result of being planted or abiding for the husbandman to oversee the affairs of one's life as one draws grace and life from the vine. In my own understanding and paraphrasing of **John 15**, this is what I understand of what being planted means in the words of Jesus. He said I am the true vine, and my Father is the husbandman, that is, the vinedresser and that every branch in Him Christ, (that includes you) that does not bear fruit because they are not abiding or being planted, He takes away in order not to taint others; and that every branch that bears fruit as a result of being planted and abiding, he purges it, that is, looks after it, so that it may bring forth more fruit.

When one is planted in Christ, His word cleans and purifies such an individual. Abiding, being planted in Christ and Christ in you makes one fruitful and to flourish. Just as the branch of a tree cannot bear fruit of itself, except that branch abides in the vine; in the same scenario, there's no more way one can be fruitful except when one abides in the vine, which is Christ. It is very emphatic for one to know that Jesus is the vine for his people and His people are the branches. Abiding in Him and you in Him causes one to bear much fruitfulness, for without Christ one can do nothing. To abide means to be planted in Him and when one is not planted in Christ Jesus, like any plant, such branch will be cut off and allowed to wither away because it's of no usefulness to the supply of the vine nutrient.

To be planted means to abide in God's word and for His words to abide in one. When we as abiding followers and disciples of God the Father bear much fruit - He is glorified. As a godly mother, realise that you have not chosen God, but that God has chosen and ordained you, that you should go forth and bear forth fruit, and that your fruit should remain; by this act of fruitfulness whatsoever you shall ask of the Father in Christ Jesus name, the Father may give it to you, because you are a planted, abiding branch.

If I were a mother, I would do all that is necessary to be planted and abide in God in order for me to flourish and blossom in Him, enjoy His pleasures, be fruitful in every way as the Proverb thirty-one woman. I would be planted in the rivers of His Word and His Church by the Holy Spirit.

There is a river of God; the streams make glad the city of God that is you, His Church. This is what **Psalms 46:4** enjoins us to know: *"There is a river, the streams whereof shall make glad the city of God, the holy place of the tabernacles of the most High".* When a mother is planted in this river of God, a door of grace, fruitfulness and prosperity are opened to achieve anything in the Lord.

IF I WERE A MOTHER: *I Would Pray Until My Change came!*

The wise writer in **Proverbs 29:15** speaks of the ways to maintain discipline, instruction and direction in the life of a child. That without such the **mother** would be put to shame. *Why the mother in this context and not the father?* To my knowledge and understanding in course of grace and time, every mother owes their child and family a practical life of prayer, for shame to be taken away from the family; only by God through prayer can shame be exchanged for fame. Oh that mothers can practically expend their energy to praying for the good of their family and household, than on unnecessary gossip, nagging and busy-bodies in other people affairs as **1 Timothy 5:1-16** brought to light of some women behaviour. I promise you, when a mother graciously prays; she can turn the hand of God to do great works in the family, the church and society. This act of a woman, a mother's prayer can be found in the scriptural example of **Luke 18:1-8**:

> *"And he spake a parable unto them to this end, **that men ought always to pray, and not to faint**; 2Saying, There was in a city a **judge**, which feared not God, neither regarded man: 3And*

*there was a **widow** in that city; and she came unto him, saying, Avenge me of mine adversary. 4And he would not for a while: but afterward he said within himself, Though I fear not God, nor regard man; 5Yet because this widow troubleth me, I will avenge her, lest by her continual coming she weary me. 6And the Lord said, Hear what the unjust judge saith. 7And shall not God avenge his own elect, which cry day and night unto him, though he bear long with them? 8I tell you that he will avenge them speedily. Nevertheless when the Son of man cometh, shall he find faith on the earth?"*

This gracious widow refuses to faint, give up and be weary; more so, she did not allow any excuses and circumstances being given to her to distract her from her intense and fervent act of prayers to the one judge who could make her life gracious and awesome again. She got what she wanted. That's what mothers can do in crises and trouble time. Hence, if I were a mother, I would spend quality time praying for the hands of God to overshadow all about me and my family until my expectations come to be from Him.

I do know and understand from pastoral advise and counselling as well as in the scriptures, that when mothers becomes intercessors, the acts and energy spent nagging, complaining, fighting, gossiping and keeping malice will die naturally. This will bring forth heavens to the earth with ease. For a life of effectual prayer according to the book of **James 5:16**, will open doors of grace and opportunities to peace and harmony to build healthy and loving homes, more peaceful and prosperous society and gracious churches of Christ. That's what I can see on how the widow and mother in **Luke 18:1-8** turns the hand of the wicked judge for her good. She refused to go weary, cave in, give up and neither felt frustrated nor faint until her desires and heart yearnings came to be. She is the kind of mother that I admire. Her intent to turn shame and embarrassment that could have been in **Proverbs 29:15** into joy, testimony, fame and graciousness.

All through the Bible, I have searched and come to know that when women, more or less mothers pray and intercede, God will not only listen but do great and mighty things that will eternally affect the course of history and posterity. I have known and seen many mothers change the course of history for the good of their family on their knees. I saw this in my mother too. Hannah is a living example to prove that prayer will change anything; it can change the bad to good, the worst to best and failure to success. This is what Hannah did in first Samuel chapters one and two with an example shown in **1 Samuel 1:12-20.**

> *"And it came to pass, as **she (Hannah) continued praying before the LORD,** that Eli marked her mouth. 13Now **Hannah, she spake in her heart; only her lips moved, but her voice was not heard:** therefore Eli thought she had been drunken. 14And Eli said unto her, How long wilt thou be drunken? put away thy wine from thee. **15And Hannah answered and said, No, my lord, I am a woman of a sorrowful spirit: I have** drunk neither wine nor strong drink, **but have poured out my soul before the LORD.** 16Count not thine handmaid for a daughter of Belial: for out of the abundance of my complaint and grief have I spoken hitherto. 17Then Eli answered and said, Go in peace: and the God of Israel grant thee thy petition that thou hast asked of him. 18And she said, Let thine handmaid find grace in thy sight. So the woman went her way, and did eat, and her countenance was no more sad. 19And they rose up in the morning early, and worshipped before the LORD, and returned, and came to their house to Ramah: **and Elkanah knew Hannah his wife; and the LORD remembered her.** 20Wherefore it came to pass, when the time was come about after Hannah had conceived, that she bare a son, **and called his name Samuel, saying, Because I have asked him of the LORD.**" (Emphasis mine)*

She turns her mourning into joy, her hurt into testimony and adverse condition into fame and glory. In her childless state of being mocked and shamed by her mate – Peninnah in **1 Samuel 1:1-11,** she turned her sorrow and shame into joy and fame through prayers. The good Lord blessed her with children of which one was called Samuel. Her son Samuel became a unique vessel in God's hand to the point that two books of Samuel were written in the Holy writ while her adversary - *Peninnah* - was hardly remembered. Hannah is the kind of mother I would be like, if I were a mother.

Unlike Hannah, the widows and mothers of **Psalms 78:62-64 and 1 Samuel 4:10-11 and 17** made no lamentations when calamity befell their generation. They were complacent in their opportunity to beseech God. They were lukewarm, careless and ignorant with their position of grace as mothers to make the needed change in their time.

> **Psalms 78:62-64** *"He gave his people over also unto the sword; and was wroth with his inheritance. 63 The **fire consumed** their **young men**; and their **maidens** were not given to marriage. 64 Their **priests fell by the sword; and their widows** (mothers) **made no lamentation** (prayers, intercession nor mourning)." (Emphasis mine)*

> **1 Samuel 4:10-11, 17** *"And the Philistines fought, and Israel was smitten, and they fled every man into his tent: and there was a very great slaughter; for there fell of Israel thirty thousand footmen. 11 And the ark of God was taken; and the two sons of Eli, Hophni and Phinehas, were slain . . . 17 And the messenger answered and said, Israel is fled before the Philistines, and there hath been also a great slaughter among the people, and thy two sons also, Hophni and Phinehas, are dead, and the ark of God is taken."*

These widows and mothers did not see the need to pray, intercede and mourn and have any sense of burden when seeing their young men, maidens and priest killed and taken by the enemy. Much more, they saw God's Ark; the symbol of God's abiding presence, national hope and security being taken away. They could not see any need to lament until God brought about the change that they really needed. This is not the kind of mother I would want to be, if I were a mother; to watch evil and wickedness to prevail in the family and society when there is God who made all things and can answer prayers, especially a heart-felt burden prayers of a lamenting mother.

If I were a mother, I would pray and intercede until my change came and my *shame was turned into fame* for my child, family and household and society. When we consider God's awesome intent for our good through prayers, it therefore means prayerlessness is a bane. It is the singular reason for failure and defeat. It is the main reason for lack and poverty. It is the main reason for suffering and shame; much more the reason for murmuring, complaints and dissatisfaction. Prayerlessness can be categorized in these ways:

- Not Praying at all
- Insufficient Praying
- Inefficient & ineffectual praying
- Praying in error

To rule and reign, more or less, to be in dominion, we must not merely pray but pray much and pray well. We must pray with clean hands and pure hearts as **Luke 18:1** enjoins us not to faint, give up and be weary; and **Job 17:9** indicates also that the righteous also shall hold on his way, and he that has clean hands shall be stronger and stronger. If I were a mother:

- I must pray in faith, believing for instant answer from heaven.
- I must pray specifically, pin-pointing the exact thing I want from heaven.
- I must pray with the name of Jesus, which is the key that unlocks God's treasure house for me.
- I must pray with the spirit and with the understanding in the Holy Spirit.
- I must mingle our prayers with praise, worship and adoration to God our Father until my change comes.

Beloved mother, today, now, could be the moment and day of change; to rule and reign in Christ Jesus in the dominion that He has positioned and has brought you into by redemption. It's all by bending your knees to pray, then you can change your rags to riches and your poverty to plenty; your fear to faith, your disappointment to appointment; your shame to fame, your failure to success; your beggarly lifestyle to a giving lifestyle; your hopelessness to hopefulness; your fearfulluia to alleluia. You can break forth into God's righteousness, peace and joy in the Holy Ghost; and break through the walls of your enemies to possess your possessions in Christ Jesus when you bend your knees to pray.

There is a need to pray today. There are many children suffering, struggling and dying before our very eyes in families, communities and society at large.

The only means God has ordained by which we can tap into His infinite ability is prayer. You do not have to pay to pray, but praying will pay your dividends that no amount of money can buy. You too can rule and reign in life and enjoy the grace that is in dominion on your knees today. There is a need to pray, because prayer is:

- The believers' life blood.
- The believers' inescapable duty in Christ.
- The act of connecting and communing with God.
- The believers' avenue of responsibility to escape from a fainting and weary heart.
- The believers privilege to end all troubles, get things done and have needs met.
- The believers' avenue of exercising authority and dominion over satan and his cohorts.
- The Believers' in Christ key to access and grasp eternity.

No man is greater than his prayer life; when we fail to pray, we fail everywhere. I was raised to know that:

- The Christian who is not praying is playing.
- The pulpit can be a shop window to display ones talents while the prayer closet allows no showing off.
- There are many organisers but few agonisers.
- Many players and payers, few prayers.
- Many singers, few clingers.
- A lot of pastors, few wrestlers and labourers.
- Many fears, few tears.
- Much fashion, little passion.
- Many interferers, few intercessors.
- Many writers, few fighters.

One of the great privileges of the godly mother as any Christian is that we serve a God who takes great delight in hearing prayers and longs to answer them. Much more, cause our child and children to bring fame and not shame to us, family and society.

IF I WERE A MOTHER: *I Would Practice A Life of Forgiveness!*

Can you afford to drink medicine for another person's headache? That's what it means to nurse unforgiveness and to have an unforgiving spirit. The spirit of unforgiveness is cancerous. It has destroyed and ruined families, relationships, kingdoms, businesses, nations and even careers of some. Unforgiveness has caused many wars and destruction in our neighbourhoods, society and between various factions of nations, continents and the people. The irony is that unforgiveness hurts and hunts the one who chooses not to forgive much more than the one who has not been forgiven. It can lead to bitterness, depression, mental or psychiatric problems, physical sickness and even murder and national collapse and colossal.

It's for this note that Apostle Paul writing in **Philippians 4:1-3** pleads strongly with two women - *Euodia and Syntyche* - to see the need to make up their differences. He even requests another woman - *Syzygus* - to assist in them making up so that their usefulness would not be tarnished as result of unforgiveness, which eventually will leads to bitterness and murder.

> **Philippians 4:1-3** *"My dear, dear friends! I love you so much. I do want the very best for you. You make me feel such joy, fill me with such pride. Don't waver. Stay on track, steady in God.* **I urge Euodia and Syntyche to iron out their differences and make up. God doesn't want his children holding grudges.** *And, oh, yes,* **Syzygus***, since you're right there to help them work things out, do your best with them. These* **women** *worked for the Message hand in hand with Clement and me, and with the other veterans—worked as hard as any of us. Remember, their names are also in the Book of Life." (**The Message Bible***: **Copyright © 1993, 1994, 1995, 1996, 2000, 2001, 2002 by Eugene H. Peterson)**

An unforgiving spirit act generates a very strong emotion that can destabilise one; and can lead to various evil thoughts and assumptions. One of such is to take revenge and that can even lead to nursing the act of murder. For the scriptures says that he that hates his brother is a murderer, meaning just for the nursing alone, one is already a murderer as far as the Lord and His words are concerned; such act of being a murderer before even the very act is as found in **1 John 3:13-15,** which says *"Marvel not, my brethren, if the world hate you. 14 We know that we have passed from death unto life, because we love the brethren. He that loveth not his brother abideth in death. 15* **Whosoever hateth his brother is a murderer:** *and ye know that no murderer hath eternal life abiding in him."*

If I were a mother, I would live to forgive as Christ has forgiven me, so that my children can appreciate the worth of life. Forgiveness will always bring forth wellness and wholeness; and much more

God's gracious blessings to any relationship - *Family, Business, Career, Friendship and such like.* The acts of forgiveness will allow God to fight your battle for you no matter what it takes and how long it takes. That's the kind of injunction spoken of in **Proverbs 25:21-22** *"If thine enemy be hungry, give him bread to eat; **and if he be thirsty**, give him water to drink: 22For thou shalt heap coals of fire upon his head, and the LORD shall reward thee".*

This injunction of the Proverbs scripture is also affirmed in the New Testament scripture of **Romans 12:17-21,** serving as an antidote to the spirit of hate, wickedness and unforgiveness in terms, *"Recompense to no man evil for evil. Provide things honest in the sight of all men. 18If it be possible, as much as lieth in you, live peaceably with all men. **19Dearly beloved, avenge not yourselves, but rather give place unto wrath: for it is written, Vengeance is mine; I will repay, saith the Lord.** 20Therefore if thine enemy hunger, feed him; if he thirst, give him drink: for in so doing thou shalt heap coals of fire on his head. 21Be not overcome of evil, but overcome evil with good".*

Making an effort to practice these Proverbs and Romans scriptural truths above, will keep one from being burnt; they will allow God to fight for you in His terms and will light up flame against your adversary as you live a gracious life of forgiveness towards them.

Proverbs 11:16 indicates that a gracious and good woman wins honor for her husband through her acts of life, however, a woman who hates righteousness is a throne of dishonor for him, simply because she can't live a life of forgiveness, she will bring forth pain and trouble to the husband by her very hand.

If I were a mother, I would practice a daily lifestyle of loving people in spite of how they have treated me because this would destroy the root of bitterness and unforgiveness. Make no mistake, Jesus emphasises strongly in the book of **Mark 11:24-26** the important of forgiveness. He did say: *"Therefore I say unto you, What things soever ye* *desire, when ye pray, believe that ye receive them, and ye shall have them. 25And when ye stand praying, forgive, if ye have ought against any: that your Father also which is in heaven may forgive you your trespasses. 26But if ye do not forgive, neither will your Father which is in heaven forgive your trespasses".* One can conclude from the statement of Jesus that there's no way for an answer to prayers without the practicing act of forgiveness in our day to day dealing. To enable one to overcome unforgiveness, there's the need to practice this recipe of a prayer walk with God in a deliberate resolve:

- Acknowledge and accept God's forgiveness towards you.
- Forgive those that offend you with a justified attitude.
- Forgive yourself for whatsoever reason and live free.

When you keep check on these three conditions the bonds of inner peace will garrison your hearts and minds as we see in **Ephesians 4:1-3:**

> *"As a prisoner for the Lord, then, I urge you to live a life worthy of the calling you have received. 2 Be completely humble and gentle; be patient, bearing with one another in love. 3 **Make every effort to keep the unity of the Spirit through the bond of peace.**"*

Life would be so much easier in all things pertaining to life and godliness - **Ephesians 1:3**. This I would do if I were a mother - The DNA of Forgiveness in Christ Jesus.

IF I WERE A MOTHER: *I Would Dare To Believe God's Word In My Conception & Birth!*

Thanks to God for today, the advancement in medical science, general science and technology that we witness and are yet witness in our generation. In spite of all this advancement, the inherent natural fear and concern of every mother is always there especially when it comes to matter of conception and birth.

However, if I were a mother, I would believe God's eternal word as it is; just as Sarah and Mary believed God in faith in accordance to the issues of conception and birth. Firstly, **Luke 1:45** indicates the blessedness of God to Mary the earthly mother of Jesus making this declaration of grace: *"And blessed is she that believed: for there shall be a performance of those things which were told her from the Lord".* The second reason to believe God's gracious word in conception and birth is in the affirmation of the scriptures as Sarah stands in strength to the conception and delivery of her baby. She became a mother well after menopause. We see her evidence in **Hebrews 11:11**: *"Through faith also Sarah herself received strength to conceive seed, and was delivered of a child when she was past age, because she judged him faithful who had promised."*

Knowing that God has not given one the spirit of fear, intimidation and limitation but the graciousness to take courage, have a sound mind and walk in love, is an assurance and insurance that one can surely overcome the placed curse and its effects concerning conception and birth as a result of the human fall in the book of **Genesis 3:16** *"Unto the woman he said, I will greatly multiply thy sorrow and thy conception; in sorrow thou shalt bring forth children; and thy desire shall be to thy husband, and he shall rule over thee".*

It's simply because in redemption a new chapter called grace with the blessedness of God was unveiled for the new woman and mother to enable her to prevail over the curse and the accompanying fear that polices it. This assurance and insurance over fear is as clearly stated in **2 Timothy 1:7** *"For God hath not given us the spirit of fear; but of power, and of love, and of a sound mind".* This is so powerful and enough to take any godly mother out of the bondage that fears have held them with in matters of conception and child birth. In redemption Christ Jesus settled once and for all this scores of sin and the curse effect;

in that He put to an end this painful and bondage that woman have dreaded over the years as **Hebrews 2:14-15** also enjoins us to know that: *"Forasmuch then as the children are partakers of flesh and blood, he also himself likewise took part of the same; that through death he might destroy him that had the power of death, that is, the devil; 15 and deliver them who through fear of death were all their lifetime subject to bondage."*

More so, the scripture admonishes us that God has assured all mothers that in conception and child birth, they would be save as **1 Timothy 2:14-15** indicates accordingly: *"And Adam was not deceived, but the woman being deceived was in the transgression. 15 Notwithstanding she shall be saved in childbearing, if they continue in faith and charity and holiness with sobriety."* More assuredly to this whole context, that God will save Mothers in birth and give them the ability to have conception of their desired child without miscarriages and fear of life and death has long being determined as **Exodus 23:25-26** enjoins us in this form *"And ye shall serve the Lord your God, and he shall bless thy bread, and thy water; and I will take sickness away from the midst of thee. 26 There shall nothing cast their young **(miscarriage)**, nor be barren, in thy land: the number of thy days I will fulfil"* (Emphasis Mine). This means that any woman that desire to have a baby, on standing on the integrity and authority word of God, should not let any form of science, any tradition or any human factor to limit her to her earnest desire to see God's word come to fruition in her life.

If I were a mother, I would hold on to authenticate that God's word will not fail because God will always be on time. Delay is not always denial. There may be evidence within human reasoning, giving reason to doubt, but God's word is more than fact, it is the truth of God. Other books may inform you, but only God's word can be able to both inform and transform an individual beyond any human reasoning as **Hebrews 4:12-13** endorses: *"For the word of God is quick, and powerful, and sharper than any twoedged sword, piercing even to the dividing asunder of soul and spirit, and of the joints and marrow, and is a discerner of the thoughts and intents of the heart. 13 Neither is there* *any creature that is not manifest in his sight: but all things are naked and opened unto the eyes of him with whom we have to do".*

We can deduce from scripture that only God's word can give a prognosis and diagnose to the human tripartite structure – spirit-soul-body- that a mere scan, a stethoscope or other device would ever do. What it says and concludes about you is the real answer to all questions in life. Only God's Word has the ability to analyse and probe into human life in full. And by God's word faith comes, and through believing and exercising faith, people of old received grace and blessings of God in their own world and time. This to believe God's Word you can know and understand in the scriptures below of **Romans 10:17** and **Hebrews 11:1-3** and **1 John 5:3-5;** I do know that, as you ponder over them meditatively by the Holy Spirit of grace, which is of inspiration, revelation and empowerment; for He will give to you, your own enlightenment which I can't fathom in writing and at this moment.

> **Romans 10:17** *"So then faith cometh by hearing, and hearing by the word of God".*

> **Hebrews 11:1-3** *"Now faith is the substance of things hoped for, the evidence of things not seen. 2 For by it the elders obtained a good report. 3 Through faith we understand that the worlds were framed by the word of God, so that things which are seen were not made of things which do appear".*

> **1 John 5:3-5** *"For this is the love of God, that we keep his commandments: and his commandments are not grievous. 4 For whatsoever is born of God overcometh the world: and this is the victory that overcometh the world, even our faith. 5 Who is he that overcometh the world, but he that believeth that Jesus is the Son of God?".*

If I were a mother, I would not let go of God until all my disappointment and hopelessness finds hope, appointment, assurance and answers to the quests in my life as Hannah and as many others in the Bible days did. In my scriptural search, I have come to know that there was no barren woman through the bible except for one Michal, the wife of David, daughter of Saul, because she doubted and did not believe God's Word in manifestation of grace as recorded of her in the holy writ of **2 Samuel 6:16, 20-23.** I pray you will believe until your answer comes, Amen!

IF I WERE A MOTHER: *I Would Cultivate My Household With Good Behavioural Attributes And Conducts!*

The scriptures of **Proverbs 22:6** and **2 Timothy 3:15** are great food for thoughts for any heart-felt parent much more for any mother who chose to live godly by the timeless word of God. **Proverbs 22:6** scripture speaks of the need to *"Train (cultivate) up a child in the way he **should** go: and when he is old, he will not depart from it" (**Emphasis mine**).* **2 Timothy 3:15** scripture otherwise speaks also in this manner *"And that from a child thou hast known the holy scriptures, which are able to make thee wise unto salvation through faith which is in Christ Jesus".* The scriptures indicating the great responsibility of the parent in training the child and the child position of acquiring the basic knowledgeable foundation.

There was a day I stood pondering after Church services of a question put before me by an elderly African man. *"It was about a young man in his teenage years who was expecting the elderly man to say 'hello', that is, to greet him first and viewing the elderly man as though they could be mates, probably for size or height sake. The elderly man said, it's not the teenager's fault, but the mother's. According to him if his mother had taught him how to respect and treat elderly people with great regards he wouldn't be gazing at him as if they are mates".* Then I recall that charity begins at home. Good deeds and great conduct and behaviour in public life are as a result of proper upbringing and cultivation of the child or adult at home at start. That's what I learnt from my mother; and what I have seen from my mother, I have seen also in many mothers that I have been privileged to meet in accordance to the Scriptures in context above.

Today, nations are expending millions and billions of dollars in monetary terms on projects, in a bid to enhance and dignify human services in order to combat the illicit act of domestic violence, public disorders, abuses and anti-social behaviour, terrorism, evil, wickedness and such likes; and their effect on the society. When mirrored properly these are as a result of the failings of some home cultivation. When there's a failure of an individual in a family, the resultant effect is that eventually community and society are deemed a failure; the reason being that the consequences are sometimes beyond human imaginations.

Cultivation in this context is about caring for and giving special attention to an individual, in order to prepare for the growth that would be expended in life. It is about planting the behavioural attributes and tending to them, in order to improve and prepare for gracious harvest, to promote, to civilise and culture for the good of all – the individual, family, community and society at large. Though the terms cultivate might likely be more applicable to plants or crops in terms, it's also, very much applicable to individual or societal way of life and productivity eventually.

An example of this act of behavioural cultivation from the family point of view can be seen of the scripture below of a mother to a son who is to be a king, meaning somebody of important and graceful responsibility. And every mother would want to have the best of graciousness from them to the society at large.

> **Proverbs 31:1-7** *"The words of king Lemuel, the prophecy that his mother taught him. **2 What, my son? and what, the son of my womb? and what, the son of my vows? 3 Give not thy strength unto women, nor thy ways to that which destroyeth***

kings. 4 It is not for kings, O Lemuel, it is not for kings to drink wine; nor for princes strong drink: 5 Lest they drink, and forget the law, and pervert the judgment of any of the afflicted. 6 Give strong drink unto him that is ready to perish, and wine unto those that be of heavy hearts. 7 Let him drink, and forget his poverty, and remember his misery no more"

King Lemuel's mother, in preparation for her son's future position, cultivated in him attributes that would enable his standing as King. Knowing that royalty awaited her son, she gave him the necessary tools for relating and choosing a wife among women. She spoke to him of the consequence of strong drink as a king and such likes. She saw her son as her vow to God and one who would one day be a husband and father; as such, he needed to be raised for royalty – responsibility, dignity and honour. That's the earnest desire of many mothers and I can see it today in the eyes of my mother and many mothers' out there. King Lemuel's mother determined to plan for her son to succeed. In the event that he failed she would bear the shame and regrets as in the scriptural readings above.

This act of home cultivation was the prayer of the psalmist in **Psalms 144:11-15**, that God would sever him from strange and dubious children. That God would cause his sons to be well cultured as olive plants and his daughters fashioned after the similitude of a palace; such that there will be no complaint and murmuring in the public as a result of anti-social behaviour, public abuse and bad conduct that might be exhibited. The psalmist's mother knew the value of good behavioural attributes as also in accordance to the scripture as written *"**Rid me, and deliver me** from the hand of **strange children, whose mouth speaketh vanity, and their right hand is a right hand of falsehood:** 12 That our **sons** may be as plants grown up in their youth; that our **daughters** may be as corner stones, polished after the similitude of a palace: 13 That our garners may be full, affording all manner of store: that our sheep may bring forth thousands and ten thousands in our streets: 14 That our oxen may be strong to labour; that there be no breaking in,* *nor going out; **that there be no complaining in our streets.** 15 Happy is that people, that is in such a case: yea, happy is that people, whose God is the LORD."*

Today, by the act of our redemption in Christ Jesus, we are a royal priesthood of God, a chosen generation and peculiar people; and we need to cultivate how to be in the home before we go out and be such in public. This is what **1 Peter 2:9 says of you as it affect all:** *"But ye are a chosen generation, a royal priesthood, an holy nation, a peculiar people; that ye should shew forth the praises of him who hath called you out of darkness into his marvellous light"* More so, **Revelation 1:5-6 and Revelation 5:9-10** enjoin that we are redeemed of God and royal priesthood is bestowed on us by the virtue of the redemptive act of Christ. Meaning as godly mothers in Christ, we have responsibility as King Lemuel's mother to have in view that we can raise our children for royalty; not necessarily that there will be kings and queens except if it is in their lineage. They would carry on them the attributes of responsibility, honour and dignity for the good and pride of the child, family and society. There is great need for good behavioural conduct and attribute cultivation today for a better society. In today's generation, in an attempt to curb anti-social behaviour, most governments tend to spend a lot, even beyond their budget in some cases. This however does not seem to solve the problem, because the issues begin in the home, with mothers and fathers. That is where the attention and investment ought to be in order for one to achieve appropriate cultivation. Much more, with the rising trends of divorce in Christian homes today, in the majority of times, the children are with their mother during their formation age; meaning without a male father figure to help in instilling the complementary attributes for the good of the child.

The values instilled on children from a very young age count for a lot in their conduct and attributes as they grow. In the eyes of the Holy writ, a big finger points at the mother as we see in **Proverbs 15:20** and **Proverbs 29:15**.

Proverbs 29:15 *"The rod and reproof give wisdom: but a child left to himself bringeth his mother to shame."*

Proverbs 15:20 *"A wise son maketh a glad father: but a foolish man despiseth his mother."*

It is the mother who is disgraced in scriptural terms, when a child is not raised right, the acts of the foolish child bring shame and disgrace to his mother the scriptures says. I think during the formation age of milk feeding, weaning and thereafter, a lot needs to be instilled by the mothers on the child. Mothers have a lot to do in child upbringing despite the societal norms today that keeps mothers virtually out of home, leaving their child in formation age to the nanny and other strangers, just to pursue daily bread. That's why society has to prioritise the care intent in order to give mothers the window of opportunity to enable them to give their very best for their child, especially in formation age when character are formulated.

Another wise thing learnt from the scripture above to help a child avoid foolish behaviours before adulthood is not to exclude your child from domestic chores. This is regardless of whether or not one has helpers in the home or you prefer to do the work yourself. There comes a time in their lives when neither you nor your helper would be available for them and they have to either respond or react to life accordingly. Then the reality of the in-house upbringing will show in their public life with or without your presence.

I have seen teenagers, people in their twenties and even older being a disgrace to themselves and their families as a result of having avoided chores systematically when growing up. The result is that they become lazy, unskilled domestically and sometimes rude. This sort of rude behaviour has hurt some eventually, leading them to domestic violence and self-destruction. Good behavioural attributes are not simply only about doing the chores; it's about creating and putting into one's life what one desires to get out of it. It is about promoting good habits and conduct that the child would carry on in adulthood.

I have heard some people comment or ask questions like *"Why would I let my child do chores when I can afford a maid"*. Those domestic chores may be the part and path of the life skills that your child needs well enough in the course of enhancing other areas of their life, also for them to later on pass same attitude to their own children, posterity and society. Remember what happened to Isaac in **Genesis 26** and how in **Genesis 25** Abraham was gone. For riches may not abide and abound forever in most of the time as Isaac's experience and the scripture says in **Proverbs 23:5** *"Wilt thou set thine eyes upon that which is not? for riches certainly make themselves wings; they fly away as an eagle toward heaven"*. More so, because phases in life are variable and life may not be quickly in the favour of your child with abundance as it is with you and each individual has to live and do life by their own faith in Christ. Hence the need to teach your child as King Lemuel's mother taught him in **Proverbs 31**.

If I were a mother, I would teach and train my household besides their educational training with the basic domestic skills for life. Such skills as in – cooking, cleaning, gardening, financial prudence and intelligence, diligence at work, faithfulness in relationship, godliness in Christ, respect for the elders and mates and more. These and more I will teach both male and female children as I have done to date; it's worth it for posterity. This will enhance the female, to earn her self-worth in her future home; and the male for greater usefulness for self and family worth. This will be of benefit when they eventually decide to marry and have their own children. I know the benefits for me and much more for them.

When other behavioural basic acts are cultivated at home they will be useful to themselves, to others and to the society at large. If I were a mother, a godly mother especially, I would guide my household in the context of liberty and freedom with **Galatians 5:1, 13** *"Stand fast* *therefore in the **liberty** wherewith Christ hath made us free, and be not entangled again with the yoke of bondage . . . **For you, brethren, have been called to liberty; only do not use liberty as an opportunity for the flesh**, but through love serve one another".*

Being a mother means responsibility; and one being able to take on responsibility as it affects a child at any point of life. Freedom in the kingdom is not the same as human rights in worldly terms. The word of God has boundaries and guidelines for the child of God in line with **Galatians 5:1 & 13**. In scriptural terms, this means that freedom has a guarantee and an act of responsibility also to it; otherwise the child may end up in further bondage of the fleshly behaviour, which could result in being in prison or psychiatric hospital or the early arrival at the hospice due to our own act of irresponsibility as mothers. It is of this note that the Galatians scripture is saying that while we have our liberty and freedom in Christ, that does not permit us or give us opportunity in Christ as godly people, to take things for granted in doing stuff in the flesh which those in the flesh who are ignorant of spiritual things would do.

That terrorist, that gambler, the burglar, the slothful ingrate, the work-shy one, the disrespectful, undisciplined person you see - has/had a mother or parent figure in their lives, assigned to raise them well and whole.

If I were a mother, I would cultivate my household to ensure self-worth and God's gracious acts for the individual child today and tomorrow society.

If I were a mother surrounded by today's changing innovations, high tech equipment, fast food stores, divergent communication and satellite systems, Internet and social media uprisings and more, I would cultivate my household to ensure self-worth and God's gracious acts for the individual child, family and society.

IF I WERE A MOTHER: *I Would Endeavour To Keep My Home!*

Every day we see how homes disintegrate before us. The core values that make our homes stay strong are crushed and crumbled before our own very eyes. They say, human hands build the house, but human hearts build the home. A regenerated heart in Christ Jesus is conditioned to succeed. But it's individuals' choice to yield one's life to the voice of God and to make that desired godly home happen. Just as it takes individuals the enabling will to adapt, to the norms of the society or community; or to self and or circumstances to define our God given home.

> **Ephesians 4:1-4** *"I, therefore, the prisoner of the Lord, beseech you to walk worthy of the calling with which you were called, 2 with all lowliness and gentleness, with longsuffering, bearing with one another in love, 3 endeavouring to keep the unity of the Spirit in the bond of peace. 4 There is one body and one Spirit, just as you were called in one hope of your calling"*

Ephesians 4:3 above imbibes us to "endeavour to keep the unity of the Spirit in the bond of peace". To endeavour to keep, means to make every effort to look after, store, have, retain, maintain, stay occupy until our best comes; and the atmosphere we earnestly long for takes root in our homes. Jesus teaching His disciples to pray, said in **Matthew 6:9-10,** that the kingdom of Father God should come; and His will be done in our lives on earth as it's being done in heaven while we worship and honour His name. We see from this that God loves and cares about us, and that He wants us to have and enjoy life here on this side of heaven as if we are there already. In other words, we experience the atmosphere of the heavenly in our earthly domain; by such creative acts of God through prayers, we are not limited geographically from enjoying the best of God on this side of heaven. God's plan, purpose and pursuit in heaven to be accomplish in us here on earth is the kind of life and prayer that Jesus taught and left us to experience even as Apostle John commends us with in **1 John 4:16-17**; that is, as Christ is, so are we in this world.

> *"And we have known and believed the love that God has for us.* **God is love, and he who abides in love abides in God, and God in him.** *17 Love has been perfected among us in this: that we may have boldness in the day of judgment;* **because as He is, so are we in this world"**

In the heavens, there's no worry, anxiety, fear, hunger, sickness, evil and more; meaning as Father God is in heaven, we can experience His grace, comfort and blessings on earth even as Christ experienced from the Father while also on earth. He's the first beloved and begotten of us, the brethren. It's when we keep our homes in this order of God's gracious definition that we are encouraged to have the mandate to lead God's Church as a pre-requisite in **I Timothy 3:5-6** *"(For if a man know not how to rule his own house, how shall he take care of the church of God?) 6 Not a novice, lest being lifted up with pride he fall into the condemnation of the devil".*

IF I WERE A MOTHER: *I Would Crave Being Hospitable!*

Being hospitable is the practice of hospitality. It thus means the generous practice of reaching out and entertaining people friendly and graciously, be it strangers, friends or family. It is the characteristics of all believers in Christ Jesus as seen in **1 Peter 4:9-10**. We can deduce from the 1 Peters 4, that we expected to have and expressed above all things a heart of fervent love and charity among yourselves; it's only when love and charity is at work in us, that we can overcome and buried the multitude of sins consciousness about us and others. More so, we are enjoined to use hospitality causes to serve others without grudging just as each one of us have received this enable gift of love for hospitality cause, so there minister by reaching out to others as good stewards of the manifold grace of God. **Titus 1:7-9** and **1 Timothy 3:1-3** indicates that this act of hospitality was to be a litmus test mark to check and measure those also that dearly desired and seek leadership opportunity in Church life. This tells us how important the very act of hospital and being hospitable should be a craving desire for every godly mother there.

Romans 12:13 imbibes every believer to see the need of distributing to the necessity of saints and to crave or be given to hospitality with every act of grace God has bestowed upon them. In life there are needs and people with diverse phase of journey in life. We are to endeavour as godly people be the one ahead in being there to show a sense of hospitality to the needy one. Jesus emphasis it in the scripture of **Matthew 25:31-46,** of the need to practice and the importance of being hospitable when answering questions of who should inherit the kingdom of God. Jesus answered, saying *"For I was an **hungred**, and ye gave me meat: I was **thirsty**, and ye gave me drink: I was a **stranger**, and ye took me in: 36 **Naked**, and ye clothed me: I was **sick**, and ye visited me: I was in **prison**, and ye came unto me"*. It thus indicates there is a big time reward for all hospitable godly people, including mothers. This is more than being charitable because of the gracious act of godly implication that is involved.

If I were a mother I would practice the act of being hospitable. My dear mother taught me early in life the need to practice hospitality and being hospitable. Showing friends and family hospitality in our home, much more reaching out to our neighbourhood and strangers in their times of need, difficulties and during their festivities even with the little we had was very amazing and touching. Touching lives, healing wounds, empowering people is such a great childhood experience I would never forget. Mama, may the good Lord bless you, indeed.

The practice of hospitality as taught by Jesus in **Luke 14:12-15** is very remarkable example for a godly mother and how also to go about and the implications in doing it.

*"Then said he also to him that bade him, When thou makest a dinner or a supper, **call not thy friends, nor thy brethren, neither thy kinsmen, nor thy rich neighbours; lest they also bid thee again, and a recompence be made thee. 13 But when thou makest a feast, call the poor, the maimed, the lame, the blind: 14 And thou shalt be blessed; for they cannot recompense thee:** for thou shalt be recompensed at the resurrection of the just. 15 And when one of them that sat at meat with him heard these things, he said unto him, **Blessed is he that shall eat bread in the kingdom of God.**"*

The scripture thus shows how much Jesus wants us to practice hospitality, which is great deal and ought to be in every godly mothers DNA as in all women. I therefore employ you to practice the act of being hospitable. Being hospitable is more than being charitable. In Scriptural terms, it has a glorious and blessed reward for the present life and the life to come, because it's a spiritual and godly exercise as enshrined in the holy writ of **1 Timothy 4:7b-8:** "*. . . and exercise thyself rather unto godliness. 8 For bodily exercise profiteth little: but godliness is profitable unto all things, having promise of the life that now is, and of that which is to come.*"

In addition to my dear mother living examples that have blessed me and others, reading a book that enhance my hospitality in Christ, had made much more the difference. This book is called "Open Heart, Open Home" by Karen Burton MAINS. It is a very inspiring book, hence I recommend anyone with a heart of hospitality to go for it. Also, I have made an update of mine, by extracting the Bible Study on "Hospitality" by Elaines L. Eriksen on the book to enhance this book should you not be able to access the book. The study it's at the end of this book, I encourage you to study it alone and with friends and family to build and extend the spirit of Hospitality to others. I believe this will enhance your quality of life and help to overcome boredom and make you one that practice pure religion, as the book of James called it.

> **James 1:26-27** *"If any man among you seem to be religious, and bridleth not his tongue, but deceiveth his own heart, this man's religion is vain. 27* **Pure religion and undefiled before God and the Father is this, To visit the fatherless and widows in their affliction,** *and to keep himself unspotted from the world."*

IF I WERE A MOTHER: *I Would Diligently Ensure Exemplary life With Fruitful Characteristics!*

Fruitfulness is the virtue that springs up out of the grace of God in the life of the individual child of God. The scripture of **Philippians 1:11** imbibes us to be filled with the fruits of righteousness which are by Jesus Christ unto the glory and praise of God if we must be able to diligently express and exhibit that graciousness of God which is us. Exemplary life is neither cheap nor common, an only by a set heart on what Christ is done in us can one be able. And this will require a diligent walk. Diligent means to be consistently consist in that which one sets a goal upon. God only rewards diligent faith, hence to bear righteous fruit; one must be set to live an exemplary life diligently, that is, consistently consist to show forth fruitful characteristics for placement as **Proverbs 22:29** and **Hebrews 11:6** indicates:

> **Proverbs 22:29** *"Seest thou a man **diligent in his business?** he shall stand before kings; he shall not stand before mean men."*

> **Hebrews 11:6** *"But without faith it is impossible to please him: for he that cometh to God must believe that he is, and that he is a rewarder of them that **diligently** seek him."*

The great remarks in life for a virtuous and excellent woman and mother are her characteristics, that is, the good fruit bearing spirit. Her worth is with good fruits of righteous acts as in the scriptural truths. It is in the diligent walk that the heavens will pour out the graces of life. Hence if I were a mother – *the godly, blessed & virtuous woman* – my daily passion would be to pursue God continually and to ask of Him the grace to excel in virtues in becoming as - *not limited to* - the Proverb thirty-one woman in these respects:

1. Be **VITAL** as Deborah - Proverbs 31:11; Judges 4 and 5.
2. Be an **INTERCESSOR** as Anna - Proverb 31:18b; Luke 2:36-38.
3. Be **RESOURCEFUL** as Dorcas - Proverb 31:11-15, 17-18, 24, 27; Acts 9:36-42.
4. Be **TEMPERATE** as Esther - Proverb 31:26; Esther 1-9.
5. Be **UNFAILING & DEPENDABLE** as Ruth - Proverb 31:11, 28; Ruth 1-4.
6. Be **OPTIMISTIC & POSITIVE** as Mary Magdalene - Proverb 31:16, 25; John 20:1-18.
7. Be **UNIQUE, SIMPLE & ELEGANT** as Mary - Proverb 31:22, 29; Luke 1:26-33.
8. Be **SUBMISSIVE** as Sarah - Proverb 31:15, 23, 25; Genesis 18:11-24; 1 Peter 3:1-6.
9. Be **WISE** as Lydia - Proverb 31:16, 25; Acts 16:14-15.
10. Be an **OVERCOMER** as Jael - Proverb 31:25; Judges 4 and 5.
11. Be **MOTHERLY** as Hannah - Proverb 31:15, 21; 29:15; 22:6, 15; 23:14; 1 Samuel 1-3.
12. Be **AFFECTIONATE** as the Shunammite Woman - Proverb 31:20, 26; 2 Kings 4:8-37.
13. Be **NICE** as Abigail - Proverb 31:12; 1 Samuel 25:2-18, 23, 32.
14. Be **FAITHFUL & EXEMPLARY** as Lois and Eunice - Proverb 31:23; 2 Timothy 1:3-6.

IF I WERE A MOTHER: *I Would Help To Strengthen My Children's Marital And Future Home!*

The saying goes that human hands build the house while the human hearts builds the home. This means one is either adding and multiplying to build a great home or subtracting and dividing one's home.

I know what it means to wake up one day only to discover that the stinking and smoking problems in one's marriage are not the work of the devil as sometimes proscribed. Instead, they are the work of a mother who decides to involve herself in her children's marital issues and affairs. Over involvement by mothers is a common cause of strife in marriages. Do not be that MOTHER! I pray you as **Proverbs 14:1** enjoins, to be a wise mother. In that every wise woman builds her house, more else her home, it is only the foolish that plucks it down with her hands.

Mothers need to let their children leave to cleave as the scriptures says we should do as godly children of grace in **Matthew 19:5** *"For this cause shall a man leave father and mother, and shall cleave to his wife: and they twain shall be one flesh"*. When your children marry, they move on in order to define their own destiny in life and with God. A mother's relationship with her child may remain strong but the dynamic of that relationship have to change if the child must enjoy the new found place, and she can have her satisfaction of years of effort to raise her child. Otherwise, she will be in illusion according to **Proverbs 14:1** of her intent to be a wise and godly mother to build her home; of which her children's marital home could also be considered as an extension of that home.

A wise and godly mother will take the inspiration and counsel of **Proverbs 12:11** to enhance her home which is her children home. The scripture read, *"He (She) that tilleth his (her) land (home) shall be satisfied with bread: but he (she) that followeth vain persons is void* *of understanding" (**Emphasis mine**).* We can equally draw parallel affirmation to this gracious habit to till her home from **Proverbs 28:19** *"He (She) that tilleth his (her) land (home) shall have plenty of bread: but he (she) that followeth after vain persons shall have poverty enough" (**Emphasis mine**).* Tilling which in this context is the act of ploughing, harrowing and manuring, in order to make land ready for cultivation; which in other words, the act of a godly mother imparting into their child marital home the necessary physical and godly attributes to enhance a fruitful relationship. This act of till is a spiritual exercise which profits both in the present life and the life to come as ascribed in **1 Timothy 4:7-8** *"But refuse profane and old wives' (**mothers'**) fables, and exercise thyself rather unto godliness. 8 For bodily (**physical**) exercise profiteth little: but godliness (**spiritual**) is profitable unto all things, having promise of the life that now is, and of that which is to come" (**Emphasis mine**).*

Such act of exercise and impart will cause the children to fight for the good of their marital home, turning every pain to gain rather seeking a quick escape from marital commitment and responsibility that have ruined many today. The child and children will act in positive terms because their mother would have raised them to be home builders and not the foolish mother who tear down homes, war with her in-laws to ruin relationship just for her selfish gratification.

If I were a mother, a godly mother of course, I would till to build and keep building until I see that the plan, purpose and pursuit of God in my marriage are accomplished. Such good would be extended to my children's marital homes too. If I were a mother, I would uphold the authenticity of God's intent in marriage by giving my children and their marital homes the necessary counsel, prayers and possibly fasting to seek God on their behalf for good; and as I am led and instructed by the Holy Spirit to see that such achieve their desired goals in order to bring in the heavenly blessings. A gracious and godly home will make a gracious family; thereby a gracious church, community and society at large.

A wise and godly woman and mother would give wise and godly counsel as proof of her fear of God. Also as an act of demonstration of the dignity and respect she has for her husband or father of the children in her life, irrespective of how she feels about things surrounding her or her marital stand for the good of the children. This is what **Proverbs 12:4, Proverbs 21:9** and **Proverbs 25:24** cautiously counsel accordingly.

> **Proverbs 12:4** *"A virtuous woman (Mother) is a crown to her husband (marital home): but she that maketh ashamed is as rottenness in his bones."* **(Emphasis mine)**

> **Proverbs 21:9** *"It is better to dwell in a corner of the housetop, than with a brawling woman (mother) in a wide house."* **(Emphasis mine)**

> **Proverbs 25:24** *"It is better to dwell in the corner of the housetop, than with a brawling woman (mother) and in a wide house"* **(Emphasis mine)**.

I am absolutely grateful to God for many godly mothers I have seen over the years, especially my mother. When I was considering relationship cum marital life, my mother sat me down and taught me and asked me all sorts of questions that my father never asked about prior to my marriage. She enjoined me on how to stay godly and stand firm in faith no matter what, and how to do life with any woman in marriage. Well she did have mounds of experience in being with my father and keeping the faith in Christ. Knowingly and unknowingly, she must have read or been told of **Proverbs 31:1-7**. The scripture is about the wisdom a mother gave to her son King Lemuel, in making decisions about relationships, behavioural acts and leadership which is *"The words of King Lemuel, the prophecy **that his mother taught him. 2 What, my son? and what, the son of my womb?** and what, the son of my vows? 3 Give not thy strength unto women, nor thy ways to that which destroyeth kings. 4 It is not for kings, O Lemuel, it is not for kings to drink wine; nor for princes strong drink: 5 lest they drink, and forget the law,* *and pervert the judgment of any of the afflicted. 6 Give strong drink unto him that is ready to perish, and wine unto those that be of heavy hearts. 7 Let him drink, and forget his poverty, and remember his misery no more".*

Apostle Paul in **2 Timothy 1:5** speaks of the wisdom that Timothy must have received from his godly mother Eunice and grandmother Lois, which had eventually made Timothy a better man in behaviour and leadership. Apostle Paul called to his remembrance of the unfeigned faith that was in him, which dwelt firstly in his grandmother Lois, and secondly his mother Eunice. He made him realised that by their wise counsel, he was persuaded that the young Timothy has a great and awesome future, which eventually came to realisation. Such wise motherly counsel is graciously needed today to make family and society a better place to live, at least for now.

Over the years I have watched how my mother conducted herself and respected the sanctity of my marriage at all times. She has allowed our marriages, mine and my siblings', to be respected and treated with dignity in the same way that hers was respected and dignified, without any interference. One thing I know very well about her are her continuous prayers and sometimes fasting, for each one of us to succeed and do well. She is a great a model as well as a godly mother indeed, who lives' to pray that no weapon of the enemy shall prosper in the gates of her children; and that her children are taught of the Lord and established in righteousness as **Isaiah 54:13-17** indicates and imbibes in us to know.

> **Isaiah 54:13-17** *"And all thy children shall be taught of the Lord; and great shall be the peace of thy children. 14 In righteousness shalt thou be established: thou shalt be far from oppression; for thou shalt not fear: and from terror; for it shall not come near thee. 15 Behold, they shall surely gather together, but not by me: whosoever shall gather together against thee shall fall for thy sake. 16 Behold, I have created the smith that bloweth the coals in the fire, and that bringeth forth an instrument for his work; and I have created the*

*waster to destroy. 17 **No weapon that is formed against thee shall prosper**; and every tongue that shall rise against thee in judgment thou shalt condemn. **This is the heritage of the servants of the Lord, and their righteousness is of me, saith the Lord**".*

If I were a mother, I would likewise help to build and stand in the gap in prayer. I would give wise counsel and help to enable them to succeed and be fulfilled in their relationships and marital endeavours.

IF I WERE A MOTHER: *I Would Be Founded, Rooted & Guided In God's Righteousness!*

Righteousness is our ability to approach and stand before God in grace at any moment without shame, fear, and confusion of any troubles because of what Jesus did for us. If I were a mother I would ensure that my life was founded, rooted and guided in God's righteousness as inspiration to my children in fulfilment of **Isaiah 54:13-14.** The scripture did enjoin us on the manner in which to raise our children, which is, all our children shall be taught of the Lord. Because of the foundation that the children have had, they will have peace which is of righteousness. It also indicates that when our children are established in righteousness they will be far from oppression, the fear and terror of life that keeps many awake and uncertain in life will disappear. When one's life as a godly mother is founded, rooted in righteousness, the scripture says that oppression, fear and terror will be far away from them; Children whose teaching is founded in righteousness will have peace and not confusion.

It's clear in **Proverbs 14:34** that righteousness exalts an individual, family and nations. For that we are encouraged in **Isaiah 59:17** to put on righteousness as a breastplate in order to win the battle of life with God. You can understand that exaltation and protection is achievable through God's righteousness. Righteousness exalts anyone, anytime and anywhere. Putting on the breastplate of righteousness in **Isaiah**

59:17 as re-echoed in **Ephesians 6:17** symbolises in the literal sense the protection of one's heart and lungs – special places in human physiology. In spiritual terms, this refers to the protection of our spirit-being – the centre of our relationship with God; this is where the issues of life emanate from. **Proverbs 20:27** speaks of the spirit of man being the candle or lamp, the sensor of the Lord, searching all the inward parts of the belly. **Job 32:8** and **Job 33:4** concurring to **Genesis 2:7** bring to light that there is a spirit in man, which is the subconscious us; and this human spirit is sustained by the breath of God, which gives him life, wisdom and understanding. In other words, man is not just living by oxygen but by the breath of God, hence the need to be established in the righteousness which is of God.

Living righteously will uplift and shield a mother, hence if I were a mother, righteousness would be my goal. We need to understand that righteousness is not by our effort but that of Christ as ascribed in **1 Corinthians 1:30,** which is *"But **of him are ye in Christ Jesus, who of God is made unto us** wisdom, **and righteousness**, and sanctification, and redemption"*. Firstly from this scripture, Jesus Christ is our righteousness; meaning that God has made us in Him and Him being an example of His righteousness; and we are in Him to show forth God's righteousness. Therefore, righteousness is a done deed by the Father God for us, in us and with us, by Christ Jesus our Lord and saviour in His REDEMPTION.

Righteousness is an act of grace and not by how much we can make it happen; hence all that's required of us is to have faith in God on the done and finished work of Christ for our restoration to God in Him. That is, being able to acknowledge that Christ is your righteousness and the righteous act to God. This we do by the acknowledging of the good deeds of Christ in us; this will help us, in order to make our faith communication of the issues of life effectual as **Philemon 6** would enjoin us.

We now know that righteousness is about having a right standing with God. That is, the right and the ability to stand before God without fear and shame in the context of what Christ has done in us, with us and for us. To be with God in relationship; and also, to approach Him in fellowship and worship with the understanding that He has made you righteous because of what Christ has done to make us new creation or person as **2 Corinthians 5:17, 21** and **Ephesians 2:4-10** indicates accordingly.

> **2 Corinthians 5:17, 21** *"Therefore if any man be in Christ, he is a new creature: old things are passed away; behold, all things are become new. **21 For he hath made him to be sin for us**, who **knew no sin**; that we might **be made the righteousness** of God in him."*

> **Ephesians 2:4-10** *"But God, who is rich in mercy, for his great love wherewith he loved us, 5 even when we were dead in sins, hath quickened us together with Christ, (by grace ye are saved;) 6 and hath raised us up together, and made us sit together in heavenly places in Christ Jesus: 7 that in the ages to come he might shew the exceeding riches of his grace in his kindness toward us through Christ Jesus. 8 For by grace are ye saved through faith; and that not of yourselves: it is the gift of God: 9 not of works, lest any man should boast. 10 **For we are his workmanship, created in Christ Jesus unto good works, which God hath before ordained that we should walk in them**".*

This context of what Christ has done helps one to be spirit-ruled and not body-ruled. This acknowledging makes our faith in God through Christ to be effectual, living in dominion. One is able to bring the body's lustful passions and desires under control, thereby having dominion over sin and its effects in one's life as **Romans 6:14** do imbibes.

Sin hinders the acts of God from being actualised, appropriated and accomplished in our lives, hence **Matthew 6:33** urges us to seek first the kingdom of God and His ways for us to do life. That is, seek the plans, purposes and pursuits of God and His righteousness, which is His ways of doing life, and then every other thing that we dare to pursue will be added to us accordingly as in **Matthew 6:25-34 and Luke 12:22-3.** The sin nature has been dealt with on the cross for our redemption in order for us to live and reign in dominion. Hence sin should not have dominion over us; **Romans 6:14** enjoins us not allow it to, in order for us to effect the working power of righteousness that is at work in us. If we can't put the flesh under, there will be trouble in our ability to live in dominion. For **1 Corinthians 9:27** wants us to keep our fleshly desires in subjection and submission to the guidance of our human spirit by the Holy Spirit in order to live victorious and triumphant otherwise our faith in righteousness will be a deluded.

More importantly to this cause of righteousness is the gracious emphasis that God has on righteousness as found in **Acts 10:34-35.** The scriptures do indicate that people's limitations in life are not because of where they come from, which family they were born in or the colour of their skin or whatever entitlement one wishes to give as an excuse. According to the scriptures, God is not a respecter of person's and there is no controversy where His kingdom plans, purposes and pursuits are concerned. In every nation, whosoever works righteousness, God accepts and gives the grace to function and become in life in His kingdom. God made the poor and the rich people, but did not make one poor or another rich. Each by their choices in life functions and become what they became.

God abhors sin. Just as sin has its works and effects, righteousness has its works and effects in our day to day life too. What we become is born in the secret of our daily routine and activities in life. This is why living a life of dominion is enhanced through our righteous acts; for the righteous shall hold unto his way and those that have clean hands shall be stronger and stronger as written in **Job 17:9.** More so, **Isaiah 59:1-2** wants us to know that, the Lord's hand is not shortened, that it cannot save, neither his ear heavy, that it cannot hear but our iniquities that have made the separation between us and God; and for our sins, He hid his face from us, that he will not hear, because He cannot tolerate a perpetual and habitual sinful lifestyle.

Righteousness has a gracious work and resultant effect on us as **Isaiah 32:17** and **Romans 5:17, 21** would love one to know. The scripture indicates that the work of righteousness shall be peace and the effect of righteousness quietness and assurance for ever. As those who have received the gift of righteousness bestowed on us because of Christ, we can only function, become and reign in life by living the life of righteousness without compromise. There is no apology for that or any room to belittle what God abhors to satisfy our fleshy desires. This is what the godly mother's greatness is all about; being founded in righteousness, is the pivot that begat dominion which empowers our exaltation. God is only committed to that which He commends. So let's live and make the acts of righteousness as done in Christ in you possible, then we can actualise our God's exalted place of grace and dominion.

An example of God's ways of exaltation through dominion could be found in Christ Jesus our Lord. He is the living example of our testament and in Him we live, move and have our being. We are God's offspring in Christ Jesus as ascribed to **Acts 17:28.**

The scriptures speaking concerning Christ Jesus in **Psalms 45:6-7** and in accordance with **Hebrews 1:8**-9 indicate that He was anointed with the oil of gladness and exalted above His fellows while in humanity because He loved and cherished righteousness with God and hated sin. He understood God's kingdom plans, purposes and pursuits of doing life. He's equally rewarded of God; and being the way, the truth and the life as **John 14:6** says of Him, it is as we believe in and of Him - then walk in His ways as the Father God expects of us, then can we experience the graces of EXALTATION.

Christ Jesus in humanity, through this act of righteousness, reigned and ruled in dominion over sin, its principalities and powers. He equally subdued all things and reigned over all limitations of the flesh. **1 John 4:17** says that, we ought to be in the likeness of Jesus. Upon this acknowledgement one can take a stand of faith and live in dominion as a godly mother I say.

If I were a mother, I would dedicate this cause of righteousness in all my life such that I experience the fullness of God; and to being a living example to my children and family of my walk with God. Being founded, rooted and routed as others have walked with God and it was accounted unto them for righteousness.

IF I WERE A MOTHER: *I Would Do Life Calmly, Joyfully, Thankfully & Cheerfully!*

A few years ago my wife Faith and I went around the country visiting friends and family. Not long after we got into the house of family friends, I sensed in my spirit the enormity of the task that the mother of the house had in dealing with two boisterous, full of energy sons and a very big house to manage without a helper and still have to work, except for the good husband. What I said to her was "Just keep doing all things with joy and gladness." This must have stayed with her for the good because up until now, when we speak, she always reminds me that she's still doing things with joy. *"Pastor I am doing all things with joy and gladness, but I need more grace from God, so keep praying".*

The use of those gracious words came up again when I thought I had concluded the writing of this book. That was when the Holy Spirit was reminding me that a chapter was missing, which I am grateful and thankful for, now that this chapter has been written to make up this book.

We live in such challenging times when there is so much demanding our attention. This results in unhappy and unfulfilled lives. Sometimes, if not most times, we do what is referred to as transferred aggression. Wherein, when we have a problem at work, or if somebody else offends and we cannot cope and match up with them by whatsoever measure of standard to the challenge, we just get home and transfer that anger, bitterness or wrath on our household – spouse, children, visitors and name it. When you have a problem in any area of your life and you turn this aggro onto the husband or children. Sometimes we carry this attitude to our place of work, shopping, parties and various places, which eventually affects our altitude in life and godliness.

Jesus Christ wants us to live, do life and serve Him cheerfully and joyfully in words and deeds; also in the abundance of all things lest we serve our enemies through bitterness, wrath, clamour, evil speaking and rigour as found in **Deuteronomy 28:47-48**. We are enjoined in **Colossians 3:17** to always give thanks to God the Father by our Lord Jesus Christ in whatsoever we do in words or in deed.

Apostle Paul in **Philippians 4:4** reminds us of the need to rejoice by being joyful and glad, not just sometimes, but again and again, always. This is why the Lord gave us the Holy Spirit, to see us through, no matter how sad the cases and phases of life before us are. In other words, we should put on from within our being, joyful attitudes, for out of the abundance of the heart – *your human spirit or subconscious man* – the mouth speaks. This is in the light of **Luke 6:44-45**. It goes to show they is an expectation of God from His children hence the analogy of gracious fruits from the mouth: Every tree is known by his own fruit. Figs are not gathered from thorns, nor grapes from a bramble bush. A good man out of the good treasure of his heart brings forth that which is good; and an evil man out of the evil treasure of his heart brings forth that which is evil: for of the abundance of the heart his mouth speaks.

The Lord by the scriptures wants us to live and do live calmly, cheerfully, joyfully and graciously. It is in these acts of doing life that the Lord will bless us and the enemy will be kept at bay.

Isaiah 3:10 portrays how God wants us to do life and live triumphantly, victoriously and graciously. It say we should say to the righteous, the one that God has redeemed, that it shall be well with them, and by so doing they shall eat the fruit of their doings. Meaning, one should be saying gracious words of wellness in and to all situations. That is the godly attribute and attitude of the godly mother which was exemplified by the – **Shunammite Woman** of **2 Kings 4:8-37**. She lost her dear and only son obtained by an act of God's graciousness. In spite of losing her son, she went to meet her husband at his place of work with the other households; she answered and spoke to him calmly and graciously – **IT IS WELL** - despite her anguish and the pain of her loss. When she met God's servant Elisha through whom God answered prayers for the son to be born, she spoke in the same attitude - **IT IS WELL** – calmly and graciously in the midst of her loss. What a godly and God's Word-ruled and controlled mother she was; she ruled her circumstances graciously. Is that possible today? Yes! Jesus Christ is the same today, yesterday and forever more as **Hebrews 13:8** accorded each one of us to know in Christ.

Many want to have a great triumphant testimony, but don't want to live and do the life required to get such as exhibited by the Shunammite mother. Many will want to fight their battle with rogue words, nagging, complaining, abusing and even cursing with diverse kinds of words to express their bitterness, not this mother. She lived the words of **Isaiah 3:10** literally, knowing that God is bigger and greater than death and whatsoever that betides her.

If I were a mother, I would crave, do life and live cheerfully and joyfully as this living epistle woman and mother. This will make God's word work on my behalf and to fight my life battles in all situations. I would apply God's word to any battle that came my way no matter how small or big.

Even at the sight of death, this Shunammite mother was not prepared to make her faith cheap in God nor to God's servant, by whom God blessed her with the child; simply because she must have known that God's blessings makes rich and He add no sorrow to it as **Proverbs 10:22** made us to know: *"The blessing of the Lord, it **maketh rich**, and he **addeth no sorrow** with it."*

If I were a mother, I would speak calmly and keep speaking the same even in the face of my absolute delusion in life as the Shunammite Woman and Mother. To lose your only child, is the end of all matters in human reasoning in most cases; but to speak calmly with gracious words of victory, triumph, wellness instead of being quarrelsome, disruptive and abusive; it's the antidote to all doubts, failings, sadness and unbelief to a godly heart; the gracious words with calmness makes this **Shunammite** woman to enjoy the gracious blessings attached to **Isaiah 3:10**.

If I were a mother, I would serve my family by God and in gracious words as in the scriptures in all situations. This I will do calmly, joyfully and cheerfully; speaking gracious words of wellness and wholeness, knowing that's where my strength will come from, especially in my trial times. This is what the book of **James 1:2-4** highly commends to us. To count it all joy when we fall into divers of trials of faith and temptation, because we know that the trying of one's faith will bring and work patience. When we let patience have her perfect work in us, the resultant effect is to make us perfect, that's mature, and entire; that's complete.

I would count it all a joyful experience when am confronted with various trials and temptations. The trials and situations may be overwhelming, but let JOY flow as mighty rushing rivers of living waters. Let the graciousness in God's word rule the day for the blessings and testimony of our FAITH in Christ, which we so much desire. Amen!

MOTHERHOOD

Triumphant Reign

Its high time God's children, mothers in particular, woke up and fully arose to their God given mandate and consciousness for daily inspiration, revelation and empowerment in order to triumphantly reign in life. This will enable one to deal with the daily affairs of life and also to become and achieve what you are born to be in Christ. There are many believers in the kingdom today just going through life, merely existing, such that, whatever they may hold as strength in their lives, be it a *Job, a position, family, finances and such likes,* if that is altered or tempered with, they would crash.

But when you understand the components of **Job 32:8** which is *"But there is a spirit in man: and the inspiration of the Almighty giveth them understanding"*; also of **Job 33:4** which is *"The Spirit of God hath made me, and the breath of the Almighty hath given me life"* showing us that when by the Holy Spirit you live in God's consciousness you get inspirations, you receive revelation and empowerment to fulfil your God given duty which could be matters regarding – marriage, family, business, career, leadership, relationship and many others. Written below is my food for thought in a moment for you. Take time to ponder on it before further reading, because it will give you the awesome leverage that you need now.

1. *When you are **inspired** (God breathed i.e. with God's consciousness), you will **aspire** and will not **expire**.*
2. *When you live by **revelation** knowledge of God you will make wise decisions, not foolish or costly mistakes that is unforgivable, unforgettable and regrettable.*

3. *When you are **empowered** by the impartation of God's grace, you will make an impact in life and live a sweat-less and stress-less lifestyle.*

Triumphant reigning in life is the consciousness of God's grace upon our lives. This consciousness is as a result of the ***inspiration, revelation*** and ***empowerment*** that we receive by the Holy Spirit to enhance and accomplish the plans and the purposes of God in our life pursuits.

Triumphant Reign: *In Every Place - Everyone, Every Mother!*

> **2 Corinthians 2:14** *"Now thanks be unto God, which **always causeth us to triumph in Christ, and maketh manifest the savour of his knowledge by us in every place"***
>
> **Romans 5:17** *"For if by one man's offense death reigned by one; **much more they which receive abundance of grace and of the gift of righteousness shall reign in life by one, Jesus Christ.)"***

Firstly, I want you to know that God wants you to have and live a triumphant life. He wants you to triumph in every places that the sole of your feet will find itself. Not just in some places of your life but in every place of your life endeavours and desired goals. God would love you to know that every place that the sole of your foot treads upon shall be for your possession, and that He has given it to you to rule and to reign over it, as made known to us in **Joshua 1:3** *"Every place that the sole of your foot shall **tread upon**, that have I given unto you, as I said unto Moses."*

Secondarily, you don't let circumstances deter you or define you, but you will dare to make triumph out of every situation in faith of what God has done in you by Christ Jesus. This means that whatever it is that you endeavour to do, as you dare to take a step of faith, you shall have it in peace and tranquillity with God. He will do it such that thanksgiving of this triumph will become your day to day song to His glory and praise. It is the triumph of beauty in place of ashes, oil of joy in the place of mourning and the garment of praise in the midst of the spirit of heaviness; while you are being called the trees of righteousness, the planting of the Lord, that he might be glorified as enjoined in **Isaiah 61:1-3** "*. . . to appoint unto them that mourn in Zion, to give unto them beauty for ashes, the oil of joy for mourning, the garment of praise for the spirit of heaviness; that they might be called trees of righteousness, the planting of the Lord, that he might be glorified.*"

Now we know that it is God's will that you triumph in every endeavour. Simply for the truth that you are the reason that the earth was created and the cause for which Christ died, was buried and resurrected as ascribed in **Psalms 115:16** "*The heaven, even the heavens, are the Lord's: but the earth hath he given to the children of men*". Further reading could be found in **Psalms 8:3-8 and Isaiah 45:11-13**. It was for a new you with the seal of triumph, victory, more than a conqueror, overcomer and prosperity or success on it as endorsed by these scriptures of **2 Corinthians 2:14 and Romans 5:17**. These scriptural mandates indicate that there is a place of triumph and a place to reign in life for every child of God irrespective of gender, race and generation. This is a place into which we can all come; a place of full and abundance grace experience and God's gift of righteousness consciousness to enable us to actualise our God given rights and privileges in the kingdom, as in the scriptures.

Triumph in Christ is a done deed and is the perception and feeling of great happiness resulting from a victory or major achievement which Christ had accomplished on our behalf. It also means the act and condition of being victorious, a winner, prosperous and more importantly, being at rest and peace with oneself and being a more than a conqueror in all life endeavours. For mountains, valleys, crooked roads and rough places are symbolism of obstacles, challenges in one journeys of life, which overcoming them in all is ascribed as being triumphant. We triumph on the basis of what Christ has done.

Sometimes life may seem unfair when a few are making it yet some struggle on the day to day issues of life. The good news for you today and for this reason of this book is that God wants you to make it and He has provided for you, feet-like hinds' feet, an assured and insured footed deer like-feet to get you to a place that you earnestly desire as the Psalmist would boldly declare in **Psalms 18:32-34** *"It is God that girdeth me with strength, and maketh my way perfect. 33 He maketh my feet like hinds' feet, and setteth me upon my high places. 34 He teacheth my hands to war, so that a bow of steel is broken by mine arms"*.

Mountains are known to be steep and dangerous. The deer is an animal that is able to manoeuvre the steep and dangerous mountains in order to get to the high places that they need to get to. In life there is steepness, danger, wickedness, challenges and more. When one dares to take a step of faith to those high places of graciousness, these can be surmountable. Simply for the fact and truth that God wants you to triumph in life, and all you need to do is to take a step of faith and dare all things that have limited you by the deeds of Christ in you. It is the daring spirit that succeeds by the done deeds of Christ in you; that daring spirit makes one to triumph in every place and be set up on their desired high places as set out by God from the beginning for you and all as declared in **Jeremiah 17:12** *"A glorious high throne from the beginning is the place of our sanctuary"*.

You know that God has not given those in Christ Jesus the spirit of limitation, of fear, of intimidation, or inferiority complex, or of no confidence. He has given to them the Spirit of boldness, courage, power, sound mind and love to enable them to triumph over every mountain, valley, crooked road and rough place that oppose to their high places of dignity and honour in Christ and in life. This is what the timeless word says about you in **2 Timothy 1:7.**

Now we know that to triumph comes with a feeling, condition and state of great happiness as a result of being victorious, having a major achievement and success in an endeavour of life, what manner of person then do you want to be by God. And to know full well, that to reign and rule in life scripturally, is to be firstly and to exercise grace from a position of God's sovereignty, in order to dominate and be in charge and control. Living the life of triumph and to reign is what Christ has done for us and in us that is **why we don't just come to give our life to Christ but to have Christ live in our life.** We lost our place of reign and triumph in Adam but find it in Christ. It's not a state of the mind but a true life reality for all God's children.

To reign and be triumphant is essential in order for one to live above the dictates of the world. This is not an 'if' condition or a place to experience or enter when we get to heaven or in the next millennium, but a call for today, even now. We are called of God to reign in life on earth by Christ Jesus: *every one that has received the abundance of grace and the gift of righteousness* – **Romans 5:17**. The Church in the wilderness of the Old Testament which was led by Moses was a kingdom based on condition 'if' before they could reign as royals as ascribed in **Exodus 19:5-7:**

> *"Now therefore, if ye will obey my voice indeed, and keep my covenant, then ye shall be a peculiar treasure unto me above all people: for all the earth is mine: 6And ye shall be unto me a kingdom of priests, and an holy nation. These are the words which thou shalt speak unto the children of Israel. 7And Moses came and called for the elders of the people, and laid before their faces all these words which the LORD commanded him. . ."*

Unlike Moses' kind of Church in the wilderness, the Church of the New Testament led by Christ is not with an 'if' condition, but based on the done work of Christ Jesus our Lord. **We are made or born into and of it.** We are en-grafted into it as a result of being born of God. It is a place or position of grace wherein we are solely to acknowledge the done good work of God in us by Christ Jesus which enables and enhances our faith communication to life situations thereby living an effectual life as enjoin in the book of **Philemon 6** *"That the communication of thy faith may become effectual by the **acknowledging** of every good thing which is in you in Christ Jesus".* More so, we are to triumph in grace because it's a seal of our redemption rights and privileges as written in the Scriptures below. God had made us a kingdom of royal priesthood and to reign in life in Christ Jesus.

> **1 Peter 2:9** *"But ye **are a chosen generation, a royal priesthood, an holy nation, a peculiar people**; that ye should shew forth the praises of him who hath called you out of darkness into his marvellous light".*

> **Revelation 1:5-6** *"And from Jesus Christ, who is the faithful witness, and the first begotten of the dead, and the prince of the kings of the earth. Unto him that loved us, and **washed us from our sins in his own blood, 6 and hath made us kings and priests unto God and his Father**; to him be glory and dominion for ever and ever. Amen".*

> **Revelation 5:9-10** *"And they sung a new song, saying, Thou art worthy to take the book, and to open the seals thereof: **for thou wast slain, and hast redeemed us to God by thy blood out of every kindred, and tongue, and people, and nation; 10 and hast made us unto our God kings and priests: and we shall reign on the earth".***

> **1 John 5:4-5** *"For whatsoever is **born of God overcometh the world**: and this is **the victory that overcometh the world, even our faith**. 5 Who is he that overcometh the world, but he that believeth that Jesus is the Son of God?"*

It's for you to acknowledge it by faith, lay hold of it and live in the consciousness that it does not depend on your effort but on the done work of Christ in faith. Triumph and dominion is for us to reign in every place of life. However, this triumphant life, is a choice of life that every individual has to make; that is, as to what sort or kind of life they want to have. Is it a life of triumph that's born from the act of Christ or otherwise!

Diverse Kinds of Life: *Your choice to make!*

The Scripture of **James 3:13-15** speaks of the various ways that people can respond to life. It also speaks of ways of living well and living wisely as its written *"Who is a **wise man and endued with knowledge** among you? let him shew out of a good conversation his works with **meekness of wisdom**. But if ye have **bitter envying and strife in your hearts**, glory not, and lie not against the truth. This **wisdom** descendeth not from **ABOVE**, but is **EARTHY, SENSUAL, DEVILISH**. For where envying and strife is, **there is confusion and every evil work**. But the wisdom that is from **ABOVE** is first **pure, then peaceable, gentle, and easy to be entreated, full of mercy and good fruits, without partiality, and without hypocrisy. And the fruit of righteousness is sown in peace** by them that make peace".* The wisdom from above as in **James 3:13-15** speaks of ways of living well and living wisely. In order to be wise one needs to be humble. Those who are envious and self-seeking and twist the truth to suit their doings have the kind of wisdom that is said to be *earthly, unspiritual, sensual* and even *demonic*. With envy and strife come confusion and evil work. But the wisdom that is from *above* is first pure, then peaceable, gentle and easy to be entreated, full of mercy and good fruits, without partiality and without hypocrisy. The fruit of righteousness is sown in peace by those that make peace. The only wisdom of great choice that is gracious and heart-felt is results orientated.

> **Romans 5:17** *"For if by one man's offense death reigned by one; **much more they which receive abundance of grace and of the gift of righteousness shall reign in life by one, Jesus Christ)"***

> **Revelation 5:9-10** scripture also says *"And they sung a new song, saying, Thou art worthy to take the book, and to open the*

*seals thereof: for thou wast slain, and hast **redeemed us** to God by thy blood out of every kindred, and tongue, and people, and nation; **And hast made us unto our God kings and priests: and we shall reign on the earth**".*

In light of **Romans 5:17** and **Revelation 5:9-10**, we see that we have already been chosen and have been made – *(note the past tense)* - and empowered to reign in Life as redeemed children of God. Kings reign and rule in life; to reign, you must have been triumphant for a cause. This is what Jesus did on our behalf. And we are to reign and rule from our position of grace and enthronement in Christ and neither from our circumstances nor situations as **Ephesians 2:4-10** depicts. The question of choice that then comes is - what sort of life? There are many 'Greek' translated words for 'Life', but I want us to consider three of them, probably that will help you weigh in your spirit man – *subconscious person* - what kind of life you've been living and how to consider what is expected of you to make you reign and rule in life in all things and over all circumstances.

a. Zoe Life (Grk): Eternal Life – *The God kind of life!*

The Zoe Life – God kind of life - speaks of the nature, life and person of God, which is eternal life. This is the sort of life that is lived with the concept of God – living the life from ABOVE as indicated earlier in **James 3:13-15**. This life is boldly ascertained by Christ when He said in **John 10:10** that *"The thief cometh not, but for to steal, and to kill, and to destroy: I am come that they might have life, and that they might have it more abundantly"* and also affirmed in the epistles as accorded in **1 John 5:11-12** of such kind of life being given to us and which is first of God through Christ to us in redemption: *"And this is the record, that God hath given to us eternal life, and this life is in his Son; He that hath the Son hath life: and he that hath not the Son of God hath not life"*.

The kind of life that God offers is embedded in us through Christ Jesus when we are born into the kingdom as accorded in our

REDEMPTION. **2 Corinthians 4:10-11** affirms this: *"Always bearing about in the body the dying of the Lord Jesus, that the life also of Jesus might be made manifest in our body. For we which live are always delivered unto death for Jesus' sake, that the life also of Jesus might be made manifest in our mortal flesh".*

This God given kind of life will invariably affect the way we speak and what we say, how we act and how we do things, view things and conclude on things. The way we make choices and decisions in life depends on this God given kind of life in order for us to reign in life. It is the life in the realm of the Spirit – the empowered Spirit of God. This is the life that you receive – *eternal life* – when you get born of God, it is the consciousness of what you have received and have in Christ that set a new pedestal for your lifestyle in the kingdom. This life is based on inspiration, revelation and empowerment in the knowledge of God in our spirit-man (subconscious being).

Ecclesiastes 3:11 declares that God has made everything beautiful in its time; also that He set *eternity* in their heart, so that no one can find out the work that God does from beginning to end except by the spirit link and engagement. They can only be understood when considering that **Genesis 2:7** did depicts and declares that after man was created by God, God breathed into man, then Man became a living being. The God breathed being of God is the eternal spirit of God giving the human spirit the consciousness of life. This can best be explained in the context of **Job 32:8 and Job 33:4 and Proverb 20:27**. These scriptures sum up the fact and truth that God gives understanding to the spirit that is in man. In other words, the Spirit of God made man and it is the breath of God that gives man life. And this spirit of man is the candle or sensor of God, which directs his path of doing life and governing every other component of the human being.

The state of man being a triune being can be fully understood when you consider man in the context of **1 Thessalonians 5:23** and **Hebrews**

4:12. From scripture we see that man is a three part being in one: spirit, soul and body. Man is a spirit being, having a soul and living in a mortal body. The Zoe nature of God dwells and communicates with the human spirit, thereby giving life to the entire being of man. Take that away, man is considered dead.

b. Psuche Life (Grk): Soulish Life - *The senses Kind of life!*

The Psuche life – *(Soulish kind of life)* – is the life that is lived within the five senses, which is **SENSUAL** – The act to *Feel or Touch, Taste, Hear, See and Smell*. This is a kind of life based on sense knowledge which sometimes constrains us to a laboratory and scientific test and some analytical approval. This is the life that multitudes want to live and still expect God to bless it. Hence the scriptures indicate how much we need to have our senses sensitised by the word of God if we are to find the chance of obtaining God's will to enhance us and to reign in life. The five senses were made by God in His creative work. Until man fell, it was supposedly to give man free will governed by the human spirit. As a result of the fall, man lost his ability to moderate the five senses as God intended, hence the **Hebrews 5:14** injunction of sensitising the senses by God's word: *"But strong meat belongeth to them that are of full age, even those who by reason of use have their senses exercised to discern both good and evil"*.

The only scriptural way to sensitise the human sense knowledge is by following accordingly the instruction in the scriptures of **Romans 12:1-2** and **Romans 8:5-9** which are:

> **Romans 12:1-2** *"I beseech you therefore, brethren, by the mercies of God, that ye present **your bodies a living sacrifice,** holy, acceptable unto God, which is your reasonable service. And be not conformed to this world: **but be ye transformed by the renewing of your mind,** that ye may prove what is that good, and acceptable, and perfect, will of God"*

Romans 8:5-9 *"For they that are after the flesh do mind the things of the flesh; but they that are after the Spirit the things of the Spirit.* **For to be carnally minded is death; but to be spiritually minded is life and peace.** *Because the carnal mind is enmity against God: for it is not subject to the law of God, neither indeed can be. So then they that are in the flesh cannot please God. But ye are not in the flesh, but in the Spirit, if so be that the Spirit of God dwell in you.* **Now if any man have not the Spirit of Christ, he is none of his".**

The life of the senses is completely ruled by our emotions, circumstances and detects of our environment. Here carnality operates, we walk by sight as the Holy writ says and those in this realm cannot please God and cannot reign and triumph in life by God. Those who live by sense knowledge are people who live by the direction of their mind, their intellect, their emotion – the human natural influence. Such kind of people can't experience God and can't do life with God as **1 Corinthians 2:9-16** helps to differentiate. The natural or carnal man cannot fathom God at all. Only the spiritual, which is man with the eternal spirit of God living within, can know and understand God – **John 14:15-17.** God wants us to have a sanctified, transformed and renewed mind which permits His word to enable us to reign in life beyond the five senses. This is made possible by presenting our five senses to God as a living sacrifice; otherwise one would be overpowered and lose the plot of overcoming and triumphing in life.

c. Bioe or Bios Life (Grk): Livelihood - *The Biological kind of life!*

The Bioe or Bios – *Biological life* – speaks of livelihood or manner of life or behaviour. The concept of life, live within - Being EARTHLY and/or DEVILISH influence. There are lots of people today who by the way they live, seem more or less as if they are just existing than having and enjoying the very life of God. Their life can be equated to the life of plants or animals. There is seemingly no consciousness of divinity consciousness in them. The Bioe life is a life built on mere human existence, that is earthly and without the involvement of the spirit-man (sub-consciousness man) and soul (*mind, emotion, will*) in making decisions in the day to day activities and in relation to the creator God. Hence some have equated human life to apes, chimpanzee and such like; hence they go making graving images of their imagined being in form of the creature rather than the creator – **Romans 1:18-32**. For this many would rather serve and pay oblations to the creature, than paying service to the creator, thereby defying their human core of existing in creation.

This act of merely living can virtually be seen also in the scripture as written in **Acts 17:22-29** *"Then Paul stood in the midst of Mars' hill, and said, Ye men of Athens, I perceive that in all things ye are too superstitious. For as I passed by, and beheld your devotions, I found an altar with this inscription,* **TO THE UNKNOWN GOD**. *Whom therefore ye ignorantly worship, him declare I unto you. God that made the world and all things therein, seeing that he is Lord of heaven and earth, dwells not in temples made with hands; Neither is worshipped with men's hands, as though he needed any thing, seeing he giveth to all life, and breath, and all things; And hath made of one blood all nations of men for to dwell on all the face of the earth, and hath determined the times before appointed, and the bounds of their habitation; That they should seek the Lord, if haply they might feel after him, and find him, though he be not far from every one of us:* **For in him we live, and move, and have our being;** *as certain also of your own poets have said, For we are also his offspring. Forasmuch then as we are the offspring of God, we ought not to think that the Godhead is like unto gold, or silver, or stone, graven by art and man's device"*.

In this realm of biological kind of life, anything comes and anything goes with no or little value attached to it. It's for this reason that people seek other means of living life through demonic and devilish influence which could be in idolatry, magic, necromancy and such as we see in **Deuteronomy 18:9-15** and other scriptures of the Holy writ, since they can't fathom God.

In life, even in Church life, people are being modelled now on how to live, talk, behave, answer questions and make decisions without the will of the individual being involved. How can such a person reign in life and live triumphantly by God? Know today that a mere 'manner of life or behaviour ' doesn't determine a man's destiny but it's the eternal life - *ZOE - the God kind of life* in a person is what determines his destiny. In life you are either living by the wisdom of God eternal Spirit from ABOVE as discussed earlier. Or one is living by the EARTHLY circumstances of the environment or by the DEVILISH and demonic influences or by ones human SENSUAL definition as sectioned by **James 3:14-18** *"But if ye have bitter envying and strife in your hearts, glory not, and lie not against the truth. This wisdom descendeth not from **ABOVE**, but is **EARTHY, SENSUAL and DEVILISH**. For where envying and strife is, there is confusion and every evil work. But the wisdom that is from ABOVE is first pure, then peaceable, gentle, and easy to be entreated, full of mercy and good fruits, without partiality, and without hypocrisy".*

You Are Redeemed: *To Reign as Royalty!*

Royalty is the benchmark of every redeemed child of God. As a result of that, every godly mother needs to know that what was lost in Adam, Christ has restored back to us in redemption. More so, Christ has become our redemption according to **1 Corinthian 1:30**. The highlight of this royalty can be tied to two scriptural declarations but not limited to them. Firstly in **Revelation 5:9-10**: *"And they sung a new song, saying, Thou art worthy to take the book, and to open the seals thereof: for thou wast slain, and hast redeemed us to God by thy blood out of every kindred, and tongue, and people, and nation;* ***And hast made us unto our God kings and priests: and we shall reign on the earth***" (Further Scriptural Reading: **Revelation 1:5-6**). Also, the second scriptural consideration is **1 Peter 2:9-10** *"**But ye are a chosen generation, a royal priesthood, a holy nation, a peculiar people;** that ye should show forth the praises of him who hath called you out of* *darkness into his marvellous light: Which in time past were not a people, but are now the people of God: which had not obtained mercy, but now have obtained mercy"*

Revelation 5:9-10, Revelation 1:5-6 and 1 Peter 2:9-10 like many others show us that we have been redeemed and made to reign as royals. *The born of God believer is not only redeemed to reign as royal but is born into the kingdom of royalty and priesthood, and crowned with the royalty mandate.* For the position of greatness is as a result of three factors: You are either born into it, which Christ is; or inherited it because your Father has it in position to crown, which Christ on our behalf inherited; or you conquered to obtain it, which Christ did for us on the cross of Calvary, one time for all life time. Praise God! Amen!!

From the beginning, God's intention is for us to reign and rule on earth – **Psalms 115:16, Psalms 8:3-6** and **Isaiah 45:11-13**. Kings reign and rule in authority and dominion – *not as overlord on people* – but over life and its challenges, circumstances, principalities and powers; and over the domains of satan and his cohorts that intend to resist the eternal plans and purposes of God for our well-being and comforts. Reigning to set the captives free and all those whose lives are oppressed and in bondage not only by demons but also in their minds – ruled and controlled against their will by their thought life.

This is not an act of revolution, it's not refurbishment or renewal; this is a redemptive act and process of God in Christ Jesus our Lord and Saviour. It's a complete transformation or translation as a result of what God has done in Christ in us and for us even as affirmed accordingly to our ability to affirm it in our life in **Philemon 6, Colossians 1:13-14, Galatians 3:13-14 and 2 Corinthians 5:21.** This spirit of grace given to us to reign in life is not wishful thinking or mere ideology. It is a true reality of what God has promised and has done in Christ Jesus; it's for us to celebrate and live on and by it in this present life also. If you know this and live in them in the consciousness of God's grace and the gift of righteousness, you will be able to reign over all things that have limited you and rob you of becoming what God has made you to be – **REIGN IN LIFE AS ROYALTY!**

When kings reign and rule in grace all things are brought under the control and obedience of Christ. It's time to arise and put an end to all the *fear-alleluia, poverty-alleluia, sickness-alleluia, complain-alleluia* and such likes. This may not be what you are saying or confessing, but may be how you are acting knowingly or unknowingly and the aftermath about you is showing it, which is worrisome. This would then affect your life goals and pursuits. You are redeemed to reign and rule in life as royalty, know it today and start to live in it now. Pay attention to **Hebrews 3:15** which enjoins *"While it is said, To day if ye will hear his voice, harden not your hearts, as in the provocation (rebellion)"* (Emphasis mine).

You Are Empowered: *To Reign in Life!*

The redeemed child of God is born of God not just to reign but to reign with God's majestic power and authority as it's written in **Luke 10:19-20** *"Behold, I give you the authority to trample on serpents and scorpions, and over all the power of the enemy, and nothing shall by any means hurt you. 20 Nevertheless do not rejoice in this, that the spirits are subject to you, but rather[a] rejoice because your names are written in heaven"*. God in Christ Jesus had given the redeemed child of God, the power of attorney to do life on this side of heaven.

Looking and reading through the pin-hole scriptures of **Romans 5:17, John 1:12, 2 Peter 1:1-4** and **Ephesians 1:19-22** indicates and endorses that we have been empowered graciously to reign in life over all things, all flesh and circumstances that have limited or intend to limit us.

Romans 5:17 *"For if by one man's offense death reigned by one; much more they which receive abundance of grace and of the gift of righteousness **shall reign in life** by one, Jesus Christ.)"* **(Further Scriptural Reading: 2 Peter 1:1-4; Ephesians 1:19-22)**.

John 1:12 *"But **as many as received him, to them gave He power to become the sons of God**, even to them that believe on his name"*.

If I were a mother, I would crave the endorsement of God to be empowered as an achiever of the grace of God to deal with life victoriously and triumphantly in every place - not *only in some places*. It's irrelevant what or how people feel or think about it, God's word cannot be bound. It's irrevocable and it's authentic even as it is written in **2 Timothy 2:9** *"Wherein I suffer trouble, as an evil doer, even unto bonds; but the word of God is not bound"*; and the Holy writ is the **Holy Bible**.

The Holy BIBLE! - It's the only place of 'THE TRUTH'; acumen of information and knowledge for deliverance, transformation, complete freedom, dominion and emancipation. The Bible may seem to be mysterious to some, but is not a mystical book, but the practical book of inspiration, revelation and empowerment. It's not a truth that you conjure but the truth that you practice. It's the only timeless, informative and transformative book in all and to all creation – **Hebrews 4:12-13**. It's not burdensome or a taskmaster, but the liberating book of complete freedom and dominion. Every other book you read but the Bible is the only authentic book that reads you, knows you and sets you free with inner peace. Other books inform you, but the Bible both informs and transforms you. And because it's not bound, it sets everyone that comes to it in faith free from all forms of addiction, bondage and captivity at no charge.

The Bible - Blessed Information Bringing Life Eternal: Love it, read it, study it, meditate on it, you'll find peace and freedom that no man can prize you with; and as you love it, you discover that there's no confusion, burdensome, taskmaster and more and any form of bondage in it as the scripture also encourage us in **1 John 5:3** *"For this is the love of God, that we keep his commandments: and his commandments are not grievous (burdensome, irksome, oppressive, or taskmaster)"* *(Emphasis mine).* Further Scriptural Reading of some people who love and crave for the word is found in **Job 23:12** and **Psalms 119:97-100.**

You are empowered, therefore arise, go to the mirror and speak into your being what God has made you to be His firstly and to reign in and through Him; and now it's the time to begin to reign with the God kind of life - **Zoe.** The scriptures indicate that *we shall reign in life by one, Jesus Christ -* **Romans 5:17.** It's for you to take your place in Christ. It's a choice; you are the one who determines the pace of your life and not God. You can take your place and reign or merely talk about it, assume it and not actualise it, just letting the events of life take their course. This is what Adam did when he let the devil take charge. As a consequence we all had to pay the price of one man not taking His rightful place in God as the scripture did explain **Romans 5:1-2, 17, 21** *"Therefore being justified by faith, we have peace with God through our Lord Jesus Christ: By whom also we have access by faith into this grace wherein we stand, and rejoice in hope of the glory of God . . . For if by one man's offense death reigned by one; much more they which receive abundance of grace and of the gift of righteousness shall reign in life by one, Jesus Christ.) . . . That as sin hath reigned unto death, even so might grace reign through righteousness unto eternal life by Jesus Christ our Lord"* **(Further Scriptural Reading: 2 Corinthians 5:21; 2 Corinthians 2:14).**

In the preceding three scriptures, **Romans 5:1-2, 17, 21** and **2 Corinthians 5:21** and **2 Corinthians 2:14,** we can deduce two principal empowerments bestowed upon all who have received Christ:

1. Abundance of grace
2. Gift of righteousness

These ingredients are already engrafted and embedded into our lives when we were born of God. That is, when we received Christ as our personal Lord and Saviour. God extended His life – *Zoe: eternal life, the unlimited life* – to our limited life so that we can live and reign in life by Christ Jesus. It's a fact and truth that we lost it in Eden; and gain it back in redemption. We can live on it today – *It is fully paid for by our Lord Jesus Christ, Amen*. You can live guilt free and stand boldly before the lord without shame, without inferiority complex or fear in your daily life as the scriptures encourage us to embolden before God to receive grace in times of need as says in **Hebrew 4:14-16** *"Seeing then that we have a great High Priest who has passed through the heavens, Jesus the Son of God, let us hold fast our confession. 15 For we do not have a High Priest who cannot sympathize with our weaknesses, but was in all points tempted as we are, yet without sin. 16 Let us therefore come boldly to the throne of grace, that we may obtain mercy and find grace to help in time of need"*.

I want you to hear and know this also, that when you make an effort to actualise Zoe in your life and live with God consciousness in you, an ability to reign in life becomes or translates as natural to you in the course of time and potentially at the very beginning. This will enable you to dominate all that has hindered you to make all things become possible. You can then be able to reign in life in these undermentioned respects and not be limited:

- In genuine love and faith
- In revelation knowledge, understanding and wisdom
- In diligence, integrity and prudence
- In righteousness, holiness and sanctification

- In consecration and commitment
- In giving and receiving
- In hope and assurance
- In patience and temperance
- In trials and temptations
- Over sinful living and such-like
- Over anger and bitterness
- Over the detects of satan, demonic powers and principalities
- Over unsanctified thoughts and imagination that works – *in and through* – our minds
- *...And in many more such like kingdom life demands.*

FINALLY

If I Were A Mother:
What Else Is There As Virtue!

IF I WERE A MOTHER: *I Would Do Whatever Else That Had Virtue!*

> **Philippians 4:8** *"Finally, brethren, whatsoever things are true, whatsoever things are honest, whatsoever things are just, whatsoever things are pure, whatsoever things are lovely, whatsoever things are of good report;* **if there be any virtue,** *and if there be any praise, think on these things".*

What else is there as virtue for a godly, virtuous and blessed mother as the context scripture of **Philippians 4:8**. The scripture challenges one as to have a sense of purpose in one's act of thought and praise and to justify such sense with the measure of its VIRTUE content. Such measures have to meet this litmus test:

- *Whatsoever things are true*
- *Whatsoever things are honest*
- *Whatsoever things are just*
- *Whatsoever things are pure*
- *Whatsoever things are lovely*
- *Whatsoever things are of good report*

Virtue is only possible by the working of the Holy Spirit in us; He helps us to manifest this characteristic. In **Galatians 2:22-25**, we are made to know that *"The fruit of the Spirit is love, joy, peace, longsuffering, kindness, goodness, faithfulness, 23 gentleness, self-control. Against such there is no law. 24 And those who are Christ's have crucified* *the flesh with its passions and desires. 25 If we live in the Spirit, let us also walk in the Spirit".* The fruit of the Spirit is one but several seed embedded. One can conclude that the fruit of the Spirit will work in and with those who live and walk in the Spirit of virtue. In other words 'virtue' which is the resultant benchmark of our context becomes manifest in and through us when we do allow this fruit of the Holy Spirit to operate in us. These fruit of virtue are these:

1. *Love*
2. *Joy*
3. *Peace*
4. *Longsuffering*
5. *Kindness*
6. *Goodness*
7. *Faithfulness*
8. *Gentleness*
9. *Self-control*

If I were a mother – *a godly, blessed & virtuous woman* – I would trust in the grace of God to help me create and manifest these virtues in my day to day life as the scriptures have accorded us; and I would also maximise them to help me create an atmosphere which my child, family and society can look up to and enjoy. For I know that if I did this I would raise godly children thereby averting the shame, foolishness and despite that comes to a mother in doing otherwise as the scriptures below do indicates.

> **Proverbs 29:15** *"The rod and reproof give wisdom: but a child left to himself bringeth his mother to shame".*

> **Proverbs 15:20** *"A wise son maketh a glad father: but a foolish man despiseth his mother".*

I pray that you will have a wonderful MOTHERHOOD experience today, tomorrow and for the rest of your life. I pray that you will live a life that's inspiring, revealing and empowering to showcase for others in the path of motherhood to follow in Christ. This act of transferring grace from older ones to younger is scripturally endorsed and enjoined as in **1 Timothy 5:2** *"Older women as mothers, younger women as sisters, with all purity".* May our God help you and bless you accordingly.

May you always remember, knowing full well that being a mother is not necessarily about what you gave up to have a child, but what you've gained in and from having one. Hence I make bold to say to you in Christ Jesus' name:

- Dare to be a MOTHER.
- Be inspired, receive revelation and be empowered with VIRTUE.
- Excel as a godly woman and an ACHIEVER in Christ Jesus in God by the Holy Spirit of promised.

BE BLESSED EVERMORE AND INDEED!

SPIRITUAL GROWTH RESOURCE

Books & Study Aids

The place of Books and Study Aids as a resource to enhance the individual believers in Christ cannot be over emphasised as the following scriptures of **Psalms 68:11, 2 Timothy 4:13, John 21:25** and **John 20:30-31** enjoined:

> **Psalms 68:11** *"The Lord gave the word: great was the company of those that published it".*

> **2 Timothy 4:13** *"The cloak that I (Apostle Paul) left at Troas with Carpus, when you come, bring with thee, and the books, but especially the parchments".*

> **Job 19:23-25** *"Oh that my words were now written! Oh that they were printed in a book! That they were graven with an iron pen and lead in the rock forever! For I know that my redeemer lives, and that he shall stand at the latter day upon the earth".*

> **John 21:25** *"And there are also many other things which Jesus did, the which, if they should be written every one, I suppose that even the world itself could not contain the books that should be written. Amen".*

> **John 20:30-31** *"And many other signs truly did Jesus in the presence of his disciples, which are not written in this book: But these are written, that ye might believe that Jesus is the Christ, the Son of God; and that believing ye might have life through his name".*

For the Bible enjoins us in **Joshua 1:8** about meditating - *pondering inwardly-* on the Bible and bible-based books, for in them is good success and prosperity. Knowledge, understanding and wisdom are embedded in faith inspiring and godly living books available in many libraries and book stores that you can access for your resource.

Publishing and making available graded in-depth books and study aids of Reverend Chukie MORSI by **CEFMORSI MINISTRIES INTERNATIONAL (CMI)** publishing and others that will inspire faith and godly living is one of our fundamental mandates. To see the triumph, victory and dominion life of people come into reality in all their life's endeavours is our earnest desire and privilege of God's graciousness.

Apostle Paul was a man of books and study aids hence he could be so inspired to write more than half of the New Testament books by the revelations he received.

Finally, we are enjoined in our mandate to declare ALL the words of this life as in **Acts 5:20** *"Go, stand and speak in the temple to the people all the words of this life"*.

A man's ignorance or foolishness is his own mountain and danger lies ahead for all who wander out of knowledge and understanding, hence the need to be armed and prepared as the horse before the days of battle in all life challenging circumstances especially just as the scriptures below here challenges us.

> **Proverbs 21:16** *". . . The man that wanders out of the way of understanding shall remain in the congregation of the dead"*.

> **Proverbs 13:15** *"Good understanding gives favour, but the way of transgressors is hard and difficult"*

> **Proverbs 21:31** *". . . The horse is prepared against the day of battle: but safety is of the LORD"*.

Therefore create an insatiable desire for books then knowledge, understanding and wisdom will be yours as the scriptures below enjoins.

> **1 Peter 2:2** *". . . desire the sincere milk of the word that ye may grow thereby . . .".*

> **Hebrews 5: 11-14** *". . . for though by this time you ought to be teachers, you need someone to teach you again the first principles of the oracles of God; and you have come to need milk and not solid food. For everyone who partakes only of milk is unskilled in the word of righteousness, for he is a babe. But solid food belongs to those who are of full age, that is, those who by reason of use have their senses exercised to discern both good and evil".*

> **Isaiah 28:9-10** *"Whom shall he teach knowledge? and whom shall he make to understand doctrine? them that are weaned from the milk, and drawn from the breasts. For precept must be upon precept, precept upon precept; line upon line, line upon line; here a little, and there a little".*

Along with what God is enabling us to provide on this site, we urge and commend you to Christian Books and Study Aids being published by us and other genuine ministries for your faith growth.

> **Acts 20:32** *"And now, brethren, I commend you to God, and to the word of his grace, which is able to build you up, and to give you an inheritance among all them which are sanctified".*

Need help in choosing a good book or study aid - we're happy to help. Further in-depth graded resource Books to inspire faith and godly living, written and being written by **Rev Chukie E. F. MORSI** are:

*   DIVINE GUIDANCE: *Being Led By The Lord!*
*   TRIUMPHING IN LIFE: *Through AGAPE LOVE*
*   TRIUMPH IN READING THE WORD!
*   DOING SIGNIFICANCE: *By The Living Rod*

- SPIRITUAL GROWTH & FAITH DEVELOPMENT
- TOWARDS *Living Beyond Doctrines*
- BEING FILLED WITH THE HOLY SPIRIT. *(Also Included: Enjoying The Spirit-Filled Life)*
- BEING BORN AGAIN: *Your Call To Salvation*
- IF I WERE A MOTHER
- The 42ND GENERATION: *(Also Included – Delivering The E-GENERATION)*
- THE CHRISTIAN MAN: *A Godly Father!*
- IT'S FINISHED: *Our REDEMPTION – A Done DEED!*
- TRIUMPHING IN LIFE: *By The Blood of The LAMB*
- *. . . and many others.*

A Bible Study
On
Hospitality

An Introduction

Hospitality is defined as the friendly and generous treatment of guests and strangers. Our mandate as CHRISTIANS, more else godly Mother and women is to express the genuinity of the love of God that is in us to others. And I trust that this study will just help you to do that in an effectual way, much more in igniting the spirit to all.

Herein are thirteen Bible studies which will help you to gain further Biblical perspective on the subject of hospitality. These are designed to be used as discussion starters for small groups or for your own individual reading and meditation. Be sure to do the study first, and then work through these studies, integrating the Biblical studies here with the applications.

Study 1

Hospitality Defined

Life Need:

Have you ever left a Church meeting thinking that you wish someone would have talked to you some more? Have you ever left a meeting knowing you should have talked to that person who was standing alone besides the stairs?

Bible Learning:

Read **3 John, Genesis 18:1-8; Judges 19:16-20**

Bible Application:

1. How does the dictionary define the word "Hospitality"?
2. What does **3 John 5–8** say to you about hospitality?
3. What are the costs to the individual giving hospitality?
4. Why should the Christian demonstrate hospitality? **(Romans 12:13; 1 Peter 4:9; Hebrews 13:2; Titus 1:8; 1 Timothy 3:2).**
5. How is hospitality seen in the following scripture passages? **(Genesis 18:1-8; Judges 19:16-20; 2 Samuel 6:19, 19:31–32).**
6. Is hospitality a request, suggestion or command for the Christian?
7. How does the world's view of hospitality differ from the Christian's view?
8. When was the last time you demonstrated hospitality?
9. What can you do in the coming week to be obedient to God's command concerning hospitality?

Life Response/Application: (Duly Discuss)

Study 2

Hospitality and Your Spiritual Gift

Life Need:

Many Christians look at leaders of the Bible Study or Church and wish that God had given them the gifts of teaching or administration or a 'useful gift.' Then they go home and execute a wonderful evening for friends, filled with fellowship and warm sharing.

Bible Learning:

Read **Romans 12:1-21; 1 Corinthians 12:4–7**

Bible Application:

1. What are the gifts mentioned in **Romans 12:1-8?**
2. What is the purpose for which spiritual gifts are given? (**1 Corinthians 12:4–7**)
3. What are the commands contained in **Romans 12: 9-21?**
4. Does obedience to these commands depend upon specific spiritual gifts?
5. How can the various spiritual gifts be expressed through the ministry of hospitality?
6. How can using your gifts through the ministry of hospitality help fulfil the purpose of spiritual gifts?
7. So you believe that the Holy Spirit can give you power to practice hospitality even in those moments when you feel "I just can't do it!"
8. What is your spiritual gift? (If you do not know, ask God to reveal it to you.)
9. How can you use it in the area of hospitality?

10. Is there sin in your life (i.e. coveting, dissatisfaction, envy) which may be restricting you from allowing God to minister through you?

11. Get alone with the Lord and make the commitment Paul presents in **Romans 12:1–2.**

Life Response/Application: (Duly Discuss)

Study 3

Hospitality and Your Attitude

Life Need:

Much has been written about leadership, but much less about servanthood. If you had your choice for your children, would you prefer them to be a "leader" or a "servant". What does God have to say about serving?

Bible Learning:

Read **Deuteronomy 15:12–18; 1 Corinthians 7:20–24; Matthew 25:31–46**

Bible Application:

1. What did Paul consider his position to be in his ministry for Christ? Philippians 1:1
2. What is a bondservant? Read **Deuteronomy 15:12–18**
3. How does the Deuteronomy passage parallel our relationship with Christ and our submission to Him? Compare it with **1 Corinthians 7:20–24**
4. Why is this servant attitude necessary for hospitality?
5. In **Matthew 25:31-40** what does Christ say we do when we serve others in practical ways?
6. In **Matthew 25:21–46** what does He say about the occasions when we don't do these things?
7. What was Christ's own attitude when He came to save us? **(Philippians 2:3–8).**
8. What does He say is our own mark of greatness? **(Matthew 20:26–28).**

9. What is your usual reaction when asked to serve? Does it follow His guidelines? If not, ask Him to give you a servant's heart.

10. What is one way you can serve Christ directly today by serving another?

Life Response/Application: (Duly Discuss)

Study 4

Hospitality When Conditions Aren't the Best

Life Need:

How many times have you said, "If only . . ." as you looked around at your house. Bigger rooms to entertain, more money for delicate eating fare, and the list could go on. What does God have to say about what we need and want to grow the gift of hospitality?

Bible Learning:

Read **1 Kings 17: 8–16**

Bible Application:

1. What have you learnt about each of the main characters in this passage?
2. Was this a convenient time for hospitality from the widow's perspective?
3. How do you imagine she felt entertaining her guest?
4. What is the main concept being taught here?
5. What does the truth of this passage mean in today's world?
6. Have you ever been in a situation where you didn't think you had enough, or that what you had wasn't good enough, yet the Lord said, "Give"? How did you respond to Him? What was the result?
7. Do you ever suffer from the "if only"? If only I had an extra bedroom I'd have a guest. If only I had some china and silver I'd have company? If only I could afford steaks, I'd have someone over. I'd serve you Lord if only...

8. How can you respond in a practical way to the truth you've found here?
9. How will your life change as a result of this truth?

Life Response/Application: (Duly Discuss)

Study 5

Hospitality to Your Family

Life Need:

Have you ever heard comments like these from your family?

The back door opened and the aroma of a golden sour cream pound cake met my children as they returned home from school. "U-m-m-m, it's my favourite!" I heard one say. "We must be having company or something's going on at Church. Mom never bakes like that just for us!" I heard the other reply.

> *"Mommy, why aren't you nice to us when we don't have company?" a friend's child once asked.*

Bible Learning:

Read **1 Corinthians 13**

Bible Application:

1. Hospitality at home! Read 1 Corinthians 13 then read it again!
2. Define the word "love". Use a dictionary and a Bible dictionary.
3. List the 15 descriptions of love found in 1 Corinthians 13. Then ask yourself, "Is this found in me?"
4. Take each of the 15 items and examine how they can work in a practical situation in your home with your spouse, children, teenagers, or adult members of your household.
5. What do you think is the key verse in this chapter?

Life Response/Application: (Duly Discuss)

Study 6

Hospitality to the Church

Life Need:

People who are visiting a church meeting for the first time often feel uncomfortable if they are asked to stand up or wear a special badge. Yet, most of these same people will respond warmly and eagerly to hospitality. Remember the first time you went to a new church, a new school or a new club. How did you feel?

Bible Learning:

Read **2 Kings 4: 8–11**

Bible Application:

1. Write down who the main characters are and what is happening in the story in **2 Kings 4:8–11**
2. What are some key words in this passage?
3. How does this passage exemplify hospitality to fellow believers?
4. What do these verses say to you?
5. What are some things that we can do to make ourselves more alert to the needs of other believers?
6. What does **Galatians 6:10** tell us about hospitality among believers?
7. In what ways does your church so demonstrate hospitality to its members so others are attracted to its fellowship?
8. What can be done to improve the situation?
9. How can you play a part in the improvement?

Life Response/Application: (Duly Discuss)

Study 7

Hospitality to Your Neighbour

Life Need:

We've lived in several residences in our years of marriage which means having had a lot of neighbours. What does the Bible say about hospitality to neighbours?

Bible Learning:

Read **Luke 15:1-10; Luke 10:27–37**

Bible Application:

1. What are the two parables in Luke 15:1–10 about?
2. What was the result of each search?
3. With whom were celebrations made?
4. Why do you think Jesus included this information in His parables
5. When was the last time you shared a joyful situation by celebrating with your neighbours?
6. In **Luke 10:27–37** who were the people involved?
7. How did each traveller react to the person in trouble?
8. Which did Jesus consider the neighbour?
9. What is Jesus' command?
10. Do you have a neighbour that is suffering? What can you do to help?

Life Response/Application: (Duly Discuss)

Study 8

Hospitality to the Stranger

Life need:

To be all alone by choice is one case, but to be all alone in a crowd is another story. How often have we met strangers to us and our circle of friends? How did you feel? What could you have done to help them and what should you have done?

Bible Learning:

Read **Genesis 18:1–8**

Bible Application:

1. Read **Genesis 18:1–8**. What is happening in this story?
2. After reading verse one, why do you think Abraham might have been justified in not showing hospitality to these strangers?
3. What are some phrases that tell us about the nature of Abraham's character?
4. How do Abraham and Sarah demonstrate hospitality?
5. What does the New Testament say we are to learn from this story? (**Hebrew 13:2**)
6. Paraphrase the story into a modern day situation.
7. What can we do to show hospitality to strangers?

Life Response/Application: (Duly Discuss)

Study 9

Hospitality to Your Enemy

Life Need:

Show hospitality to my family, my church, my neighbours and strangers, okay! But to my enemy? Isn't that pushing it?

Bible Learning:

Read **Proverbs 25:21–22; Matthew 5:41–48; Romans 12: 9-21** and **2 Kings 6:18–23**

Bible Application:

1. Read **Proverbs 25:21–22, Matthew 5:41–44** and **Romans 12:9-21** and list the commands in these verses
2. What is the promise contained in these passages?
3. History tells us that to give someone a coal of fire would be skin to "giving a light" in a day when matches and a lighter fluid were not prevalent. What is the meaning of "heaping coals of fire" on your enemy? (**John 18:18**)
4. Read **2 Kings 6:18–23**. What was the result of Elisha's hospitality to the Syrians?
5. What lesson can we learn from this story?
6. If you feel that there are people that you just can't love, what does the Lord promise to do? (**Philippians 4:19; Romans 8:1–16; Romans 12:9-21**).
7. Who do you know that you need to "heap coals of fire" upon and love to Jesus, not in your own strength but in His?

Life Response/Application: (Duly Discuss)

Study 10

Hospitality in Your Home

Life Need:

Have you ever thought about the purpose of your house? Most of us view it as a shelter for the family or a focal point for family activist. How else could it be used?

Bible Learning:

Read **Acts 16:13 – 15; Matthew 10:20–42, Acts 28:30-32**

Bible Application:

1. Tell the story in **Acts 16:13–15** in your own words, answering the questions who, what, when, where and how.
2. What did Lydia offer Paul and Luke and why?
3. For what purpose was the home used in **Acts 5:42**?
4. Why did salvation of the Gentiles make the command to practise hospitality ungrudgingly more important?
5. Today we have numerous large church buildings. How can we still use our homes?
6. What is Jesus saying to us in **Matthew 10:40–42** concerning our homes and hospitality?
7. What does **Acts 28:30–31** tell us about Paul's hospitality?
8. What were Paul's living conditions?
9. Have you ever said, "I'd open my home if only it were larger, or if only I had nicer things?" Are you willing to give your home to the Lord for His use, no matter how large or small it is?

Life Response/Application: (Duly Discuss)

Study 11

Hospitality through Your Finances

Life Need:

When you think about the cost of hospitality, do you think first about time or money? Hospitality sometimes costs both. What does the Bible say about money?

Bible Learning:

Read **Luke 6:38; Matthew 6:19–21; Matthew 25:14–30**

Bible Applications:

1. What does money have to do with hospitality?
2. What does the Bible say about money?
3. How does money relate to the ministry of hospitality?
4. Did Jesus talk about money? Read **Matthew 25:14–30**
5. Who is the owner of all? Why?
6. What is my responsibility as a steward?
7. Is spending money for hospitality good stewardship? Why or why not?
8. Do you hold all that He has entrusted you with an open hand thus enabling Him to add or take away at will?
9. What is the difference between just making out a cheque and giving thorough hospitality?
10. What are some practical ways you are (or could be) showing financial hospitality?

Life Response/Application: (Duly Discuss)

Study 12

Hospitality through Your Time

Life Need:

At this point in the study you might be saying, "I really don't have a whole lot of money or much of a house for hospitality." Maybe you're still living in a dorm room or in someone else's home. Then what about time? What do you do with the 24 hours in each day?

Bible Learning:

Read **Mark 6:7–10, 10:13–16; John 11:1-45; Luke 10:38-42**

Bible Application:

1. Jesus sends out His disciples. What are His instructions?
2. What did they have to give?
3. Do you take time to STOP and listen when a friend needs to share, your little one wants to tell you of his big adventure, or your teenager of her greatest conflict, or your spouse of his goals and dreams?
4. Read **John 11:1–45**. Could Jesus have performed the same miracle from afar?
5. Why did Jesus take the time to go to the home of Mary and Martha?
6. In **Luke 10:38–42** contrast Martha's hospitality of her home with Mary's hospitality of her time
7. What can you learn from this?
8. Look at **Mark 10:13–16**. Who did Jesus have time for here?
9. What special things did He do with the children?

10. What are some other examples of the use of time in hospitality given in the Bible?

11. Do you have time for Hospitality or is your schedule too complicated? What can you do to better organize your time?

Life Response/Application: (Duly Discuss)

Study 13

Hospitality: How Do You Handle It?

Life Need:

Have you ever rejected someone hospitality? Or, have you ever wanted to show hospitality, but then backed off because you were afraid you might be turned down? How did you feel later? Do you wish you had made a different decision?

Bible Learning:

Read **John 13:3–9**

Bible Application:

1. Who was offering hospitality and who was on the receiving end?
2. Why was it so difficult for Peter to let Christ serve him?
3. Can apparent humility such as Peter's actually be pride? If so, in what way?
4. Why was it important for Peter to accept what Jesus had offered?
5. Why do people find it difficult to receive when others offer hospitality?
6. How do you react when others reject your hospitality?
7. What can you do to put people at ease so that they will be more receptive to hospitality?

Life Response/Application: (Duly Discuss)

SCRIPTURAL READING

Luke 1:_45 "And **blessed is she that believed** for there shall be a performance of those things which were told her from the Lord."_

Proverb 14:1 _"Every **wise woman** buildeth her house: but the foolish plucketh it down with her hands."_

Proverb 24:3-4 _"Through **wisdom** is a house built; and by **understanding** it is established: And by **knowledge** shall the chambers be filled with all precious and pleasant riches."_

Proverb 29:15 _"The **rod and reproof** give wisdom: **but a child left to himself bringeth his mother to shame.**"_

Proverbs 15:20 _"A wise **son** maketh a glad father: but a foolish **man** despiseth his **mother.**"_

Proverbs 22:6 _"Train up a **child** in the way he should go: and when he is old, he will not depart from it."_

2 Timothy 3:15 _"And that from a **child** thou hast known the holy scriptures, which are able to make thee wise unto salvation through faith which is in Christ Jesus."_

Proverbs 31:1-31 _"The words of **king Lemuel**, the prophecy that **his mother taught him. 2What, my son? and what, the son of my womb? and what, the son of my vows?** 3Give not thy strength unto women, nor thy ways to that which destroyeth kings. 4It is not for kings, O Lemuel, it is not for kings to drink wine; nor for princes strong drink: 5Lest they drink, and forget the law, and pervert the judgment of any of the afflicted. 6Give_ *strong drink unto him that is ready to perish, and wine unto those that be of heavy hearts. 7Let him drink, and forget his poverty, and remember his misery no more. 8Open thy mouth for the dumb in the cause of all such as are appointed to destruction. 9Open thy mouth, judge righteously, and plead the cause of the poor and needy. 10Who* **can find a virtuous woman? for her price is far above rubies.** *11The heart of her husband doth safely trust in her, so that he shall have no need of spoil. 12She will do him good and not evil all the days of her life. 13She seeketh wool, and flax, and worketh willingly with her hands. 14She is like the merchants' ships; she bringeth her food from afar. 15She riseth also while it is yet night, and giveth meat to her household, and a portion to her maidens. 16She considereth a field, and buyeth it: with the fruit of her hands she planteth a vineyard. 17She girdeth her loins with strength, and strengtheneth her arms. 18She perceiveth that her merchandise is good:* **her candle goeth not out by night.** *19She layeth her hands to the spindle, and her hands hold the distaff. 20She stretcheth out her hand to the poor; yea, she reacheth forth her hands to the needy. 21She is not afraid of the snow for her household: for all her household are clothed with scarlet. 22She maketh herself coverings of tapestry; her clothing is silk and purple. 23Her husband is known in the gates, when he sitteth among the elders of the land. 24She maketh fine linen, and selleth it; and delivereth girdles unto the merchant.* **25Strength and honour are her clothing;** *and she shall rejoice in time to come.* **26She openeth her mouth with wisdom;** *and in her tongue is the law of kindness. 27She looketh well to the ways of her household, and eateth not the bread of idleness. 28Her children arise up, and call her* **blessed;** *her husband also, and he* **praiseth** *her. 29Many* **daughters have done virtuously, but thou excellest them all.** *30Favour is deceitful, and beauty is vain:* **but a woman that feareth the LORD, she shall be praised.** *31Give her of the fruit of her hands; and* **let her own works praise her in the gates.***"

Matthew 6:25-34 *"Therefore I say unto you, Take no thought for your life, what ye shall eat, or what ye shall drink; nor yet for your body, what ye shall put on. Is not the life more than meat, and the body than raiment? 26 Behold the fowls of the air: for they sow not, neither do they reap, nor gather into barns; yet your heavenly Father feedeth them. Are ye not much* *better than they? 27* **Which of you by taking thought can add one cubit unto his stature?** *28 And why take ye thought for raiment? Consider the lilies of the field, how they grow; they toil not, neither do they spin: 29 and yet I say unto you, That even Solomon in all his glory was not arrayed like one of these. 30 Wherefore, if God so clothe the grass of the field, which to day is, and to morrow is cast into the oven, shall he not much more clothe you, O ye of little faith? 31 Therefore take no thought, saying, What shall we eat? or, What shall we drink? or, Wherewithal shall we be clothed? 32 (For after all these things do the Gentiles seek:)* **for your heavenly Father knoweth that ye have need of all these things. 33 But seek ye first the kingdom of God, and his righteousness; and all these things shall be added unto you.** *34 Take therefore no thought for the morrow: for the morrow shall take thought for the things of itself. Sufficient unto the day is the evil thereof."*

Luke 12:22-33 *"And he said unto his disciples, Therefore I say unto you, Take no thought for your life, what ye shall eat; neither for the body, what ye shall put on. 23 The life is more than meat, and the body is more than raiment. 24 Consider the ravens: for they neither sow nor reap; which neither have storehouse nor barn; and God feedeth them: how much more are ye better than the fowls? 25 And which of you with taking thought can add to his stature one cubit? 26 If ye then be not able to do that thing which is least, why take ye thought for the rest? 27 Consider the lilies how they grow: they toil not, they spin not; and yet I say unto you, that Solomon in all his glory was not arrayed like one of these. 28 If then God so clothe the grass, which is to day in the field, and to morrow is cast into the oven; how much more will he clothe you, O ye of little faith? 29 And seek not ye what ye shall eat, or what ye shall drink, neither be ye of doubtful mind.* **30 For all these things do the nations of the world seek after: and your Father knoweth that ye have need of these things. 31 But rather seek ye the kingdom of God; and all these things shall be added unto you. 32 Fear not, little flock; for it is your Father's good pleasure to give you the kingdom.** *33 Sell that ye have, and give alms; provide yourselves bags which wax not old, a treasure in the heavens that faileth not, where no thief approacheth, neither moth corrupteth."*

1 Thessalonians 5:23 *"And the very God of peace sanctify you wholly; and I pray God your* **whole spirit and soul and body** *be preserved blameless unto the coming of our Lord Jesus Christ."*

Hebrews 4:12 *"For the word of God is quick, and powerful, and sharper than any twoedged sword, piercing even to the dividing asunder of* **soul and spirit, and of the joints and marrow***, and is a discerner of the thoughts and intents of the heart."*

THE LAST WORDS

Your Salvation

Being Born Again

To being 'Born Again' thus means to Being Born from above; which is of and with God's nature. That's what makes the believer in Christ Jesus a New Creation even as it's written in **John 3:3-8** and **2 Corinthians 5:17**.

Scriptural Reading:

Read **John 3:3-8, 16-18; 2 Corinthians 5:17; Romans 10:8-13, Proverbs 28:13; 1 Peter 1:23; Titus 2:11-15**.

1. **Acknowledge** that you are a sinner - **Psalm 57:2-3**.
2. **Believe** in your heart on God's provision for your sinful nature forgiveness and triumph, through Jesus Christ in His Blood - **Romans 10:10-13; Acts 4:12; 1 Timothy 2:15; Hebrews 9:12**.
3. **Repent** (i.e. renounce) from sin and satan in your life and confess Jesus Christ as your personal Saviour and Lord - **Proverbs 28:13; Romans 10:8-13; Acts 17:30-31, 20:21**.
4. **Appropriate** by faith your rights into the Redemption provisions of God for you in Christ Jesus – **2 Corinthians 5:17-21; Romans 10:8-10; Colossians 1:13-14; Hebrews 11:1, 6; Ephesian 1:7**.
5. **Go forth** in Faith through consistent study the WORD (Bible), Pray, Fellowship with Christians of like faith, &

Testify your faith to others, thereby enjoying eternal life by the help of the Holy Spirit provisions - **Hebrews 10:25; Romans 8:14-16; John 8:30-32; 2 Timothy 3:15; John 15:17.**

For further spiritual growth especially on this this topic, endeavour to get and read my book entitled: *"Towards Being Born Again"*

Further Contacts:

Email Address:

pstchukie@42ndgenerationfoundation.com

Websites:

www.cefmorsiministriesinternational.com
www.42ndgenerationfoundation.com
www.achieversfaithdigest.com
www.redemptionlifeinternational.org

Telephone:

(+44) 07463666227
(+44) 07748375997
(+44) 01179506853

Write today to:

CEFMORSI MINISTRIES INTERNATIONAL
39 Marlwood Drive, Brentry, Bristol
BS10 6SH. England, United Kingdom.

**You are welcome to attend our Kingdom-
Church Growth Schools, Seminars, Conferences
and Conventions where necessary**

Chukie E. F. MORSI is the Setman, Founder and Visioneer of **CEFMORSI MINISTRIES INTERNATIONAL**, which oversees the 42nd Generation Foundation (*His Global Outreach Mission Platform*). He is the Custodian and Publisher of Achievers' FAITH Digest (*A Monthly TEACHING Publication*) and the Presiding Pastor of Redemption Life International Churches (*The Community Liaison Platform*). He is the Chairman of CEFMORSI INTERNATIONAL (*Achievers' FAITH Commendation Bureau*).

He is a born again, Spirit-filled, seasoned and anointed servant of God; A prophetic teacher in ministry and a missionary pastor by calling. As a charismatic and dynamic testament minister, he is a called servant of God, set apart, ordained and commissioned in response to his love for God and the commitment for the redemption of mankind.

He is a former graduate of mechanical engineering, who received the call of God to an Apostolic Ministry in 1983. He eventually answered that call in 1994 while on the verge of pursuing his engineering career in the oil industry.

He is married to Faith and blessed with five wonderful children - Daniel, Joshua, Emmanuella, Joel and Zachary and they live in Bristol, England.

He has written and authored some Bible Teaching Manuals for Church Services. Now His inspiring, revealing and empowering books and others are being published; among are these most desired and entitled: Divine Guidance - *Being Led By The Lord!*; Triumphing In Life - *Through AGAPE LOVE*; The 42ⁿᵈ Generation - A People of *Hope, Faith & Love*; DOING SIGNIFICANCE - *By The Living Rod*; Spiritual Growth & Faith Development; TOWARDS - *Living Beyond Doctrines*; BEING FILLED WITH THE HOLY SPIRIT - Enjoying The Spirit-Filled Life; Being Born Again - Your Call To Salvation; Faith In God's Anointed; TRIUMPH! *Reading The WORD*; The Christian Man: *Being A Godly Father and* many others.